HANDBOOK TO
INTERACTIVE BIBLE STUDY

DENNIS FLEDDERJOHANN

Design by the vg-r collective (www.vg-r.com).
Printed in the United States of America.

ISBN 978-0-615-31980-3

CONTENTS

WORKSHEETS ONLINE

All of the worksheets in the book are available as full-sheet versions at the book web site. You can use these versions in the classroom or for your own study.

www.dennisfledderjohann.com

INTRODUCTION

In church meetings, I often find myself looking at members of the Body of Christ around me. I see brothers and sisters who are dealing with big battles in their lives—some with diseases, others experiencing great stress and pain. The Christian life is not easy; it is sometimes challenging and overwhelming. Yet I wonder, how often do I place myself in painful circumstances because I fail to be obedient to God and His Word? And when I have failed, is it because I do not *know* God's Word? Is my weakness a result of my failure to *respond to* the Truth of the Word?

In the Middle Ages[1], Jews were accused of starting and perpetuating the Black Plague, the dread disease that killed young and old, rich and poor, male and female alike. Yet the Jews as a people were spared this fate. Why? Because they were obedient to the sanitation rules of the Levitical law found in the Old Testament.

Identity is a personal, life-long struggle for me. Again and again I find that it is so much easier to identify with what I do, my behavior, my occupation, my calling—something that people can see; it is concrete, down-to-earth. How does my understanding of being "in Christ" communicate to others? How do I explain that I am the Dennis form of Christ on this earth? I often wonder if I really understand it beyond the surface level, let alone attempt to explain it to others. This struggle with

---

1. Black, Jacquedyn G. *Microbiology: Principles and Exploration.* 5th edition, John Wiley and Sons, New York, NY, 2002, pp. 10-11.

my identity in Christ and understanding the implications is explained in Colossians 3:1-4 when it reaches a climax of "life in Christ." Will I ever fully understand this? My failures and inadequacies drive me back to the Word. Bible study is for life.

Bible study is not popular. In a day of pleasure, comfort, and immediacy, it is hard work. If it is your desire to know God, the study of His Word is essential. Desire is not enough; it must be followed by action. There are several prerequisites to deep study of the Bible that will provide relevant, life giving, and spiritually nourishing truths to help transform your life in this fallen world.

1. **Regeneration.** The Bible cannot truly be understood unless the regenerating work of the Holy Spirit has taken place in one's life. Life in Christ grows this understanding of the Word and the sanctification process within the thought life.

2. **Confidence in the Scriptures.** The Bible must be accepted as the inspired Word of God. Though many have criticized and rejected the Bible as God's Word, openhearted Bible study places confidence that the Bible is, indeed, God's Word.

3. **Dependence upon the Holy Spirit.** The Holy Spirit is our Teacher who will guide us into Truth, opening our eyes and minds to His directions.

4. **Obedience.** Without a positive response to God's Word, Bible study fails to bring life changes. Knowing and acting upon the Truth are not synonymous, although knowing needs to lead to action.

People have various motives for studying the Bible. For some, the motivation is to understand the historical context of Judaism and later, Christianity, or to learn how people lived many years ago, or how the world began, or how to pray. Yet, at some point I believe the Holy Spirit convicts us that our study of the Bible is to know the God of the Bible, and to more fully and personally know who He is and the kingdom He is building. In this process we become conformed to His image, as the Word is internalized, obeyed, and applied to our lives through the indwelling Holy Spirit. Bible study is building a relationship with God, which requires time and effort.

The purposes of this handbook are to present an overview of interactive Bible study and to demonstrate ways in which it can be used in personal and group Bible study. Emphasis is placed on the process of observation, interpretation, and application. Thus, a variety of worksheets are provided for personal Bible study. These may be copied and used! Optional assignments are found within and at the end of each chapter.

It is my desire to motivate interested and willing students of the English Bible to learn how to study and learn God's Truth. Yet, it is important to realize that God's Word is revelation, not just facts and stories. This means that I, or any one else, cannot open minds or give understanding. God's Word is revelation and therefore must be uncovered and revealed by God Himself. This process is endless and continues as one is open to the Spirit's voice and teaching, and it cannot be evaluated by academic testing, but rather it is examined by life. God, the Giver of life, uses daily life experiences to teach us about Himself.

As a parent and teacher, I believe my responsibility includes teaching our children and students God's wisdom. Bible study needs to become part of their lives, not in a regimented or legalistic way, but rather in directions that encourage their attitudes and appetites for God's Word to grow. Therefore, various types of observation exercises are included. Realizing that God's Word is revelation and not just facts and knowledge, I desire to encourage but never manipulate or force Bible study merely for the sake of Bible study. If you are a parent or teacher, stimulate children's spiritual lives so that ultimately they will naturally want to study God's Word. Each person must realize that learning about and knowing God is revelation. May the child naturally develop study habits because he or she has received a continual revelation of Jesus Christ in his or her life and in ways that the truth of Jesus Christ applies to daily life.

WHY IS BIBLE STUDY IMPORTANT?

1. Is Bible study important? Why? List as many reasons as you can.

2. From your answers above, what verses in Scripture would support those reasons? If you find a verse, write the reference beside your reason.

3. What reasons, other than Scriptural ones, can there be for studying the Bible? For what reasons would a non-Christian study the Bible? A person who is interested in literature? A person who is seeking answers to life?

4. What barriers have discouraged you from studying the Bible? Give at least three.

5. Examine the following Scriptures to determine what is said about Bible study; then
   write a summary statement about Bible study.

Deuteronomy 6:4-9	Psalms 1	Psalms 119:9-16
2 Timothy 2:14-19	2 Timothy 3:10-17	Hebrews 4:12-13

Prayer: Heavenly Father, please continue to open my spiritual eyes to who You are, and may this book be a means of learning to see You through different windows. God, increase my creativity in the study of Your Word, and may Your wisdom direct me to help others to study the Word. May Your Holy Spirit empower me—and others—as we learn and integrate your Truth into our lives. Thank You. For this I pray in Jesus' Name. Amen.

IN THE LABORATORY WITH AGASSIZ[2]

By a former pupil
Because of its relevance to Bible study, this classic story is included.

It was more than fifteen years ago that I entered the laboratory of Professor Agassiz, and told him I had enrolled my name in the scientific school as a student of natural history. He asked me a few questions about my object in coming, my antecedents generally, the mode in which I afterwards proposed to use the knowledge I might acquire, and finally, whether I wished to study any special branch. To the latter I replied that while I wished to be well grounded in all departments of zoology, I purposed to devote myself specially to insects.

"When do you wish to begin?" he asked.

"Now," I replied.

This seemed to please him, and with an energetic "Very well," he reached from a shelf a huge jar of specimens in yellow alcohol.

"Take this *fish*," said he, "and look at it; we call it a Hæmulon; by and by I will

---

2. Appendix, *American Poems: Longfellow: Whittier: Bryant: Holmes: Lowell: Emerson with Biographical Sketches and Notes.* Boston: Houghton, Osgood and Company, The Riverside Press, Cambridge, 1880, pp. 451-455.

ask what you have seen."

With that he left me, but in a moment returned with explicit instructions as to the care of the object intrusted to me.

"No man is fit to be a naturalist," said he, "who does not know how to take care of specimens."

I was to keep the fish before me in a tin tray, and occasionally moisten the surface with alcohol from the jar, always taking care to replace the stopper tightly. Those were not the days of ground glass stoppers, and elegantly shaped exhibition jars; all the old students will recall the huge, neckless glass bottles with their leaky, wax-besmeared corks, half eaten by insects and begrimed with cellar dust. Entomology was a cleaner science than ichthyology, but the example of the professor who had unhesitatingly plunged to the bottom of the jar to produce the fish was infectious; and though this alcohol had "a very ancient and fish-like smell," I really dared not show any aversion within these sacred precincts, and treated the alcohol as though it were pure water. Still I was conscious of a passing feeling of disappointment, for gazing at a fish did not commend itself to an ardent entomologist. My friends at home, too, were annoyed, when they discovered that no amount of *eau de cologne* would drown the perfume which haunted me like a shadow.

In ten minutes I had seen all that could be seen in that fish, and started in search of the professor, who had, however, left the museum; and when I returned, after lingering over some of the odd animals stored in the upper apartment, my specimen was dry all over. I dashed the fluid over the fish as if to resuscitate the beast from a fainting-fit, and looked with anxiety for a return of the normal, sloppy appearance. This little excitement over, nothing was to be done but return to a steadfast gaze at my mute companion. Half an hour passed,—an hour,— another hour; the fish began to look loathsome. I turned it over and around; looked it in the face,—ghastly; from behind, beneath, above, sideways, at a three quarters view,—just as ghastly. I was in despair; at an early hour I concluded that lunch was necessary; so, with infinite relief, the fish was carefully replaced in the jar, and for an hour I was free.

On my return, I learned that Professor Agassiz had been at the museum, but had gone and would not return for several hours. My fellow students were too busy to be disturbed by continued conversation. Slowly I drew forth that hideous fish, and with a feeling of desperation again looked at it. I might not use a magnifying glass; instruments of all kinds were interdicted. My two hands, my two eyes, and the fish; it seemed a most limited field. I pushed my finger down its throat to feel how sharp the teeth were. I began to count the scales in the different rows until I was convinced that that was nonsense. At last a happy thought struck me—I would draw the fish; and now with surprise I began to discover new features in the creature. Just then the professor returned.

"That is right," said he; "a pencil is one of the best of eyes. I am glad to notice, too, that you keep your specimen wet and your bottle corked."

With these encouraging words, he added,—

"Well, what is it like?"

He listened attentively to my brief rehearsal of the structure of parts whose names were still unknown to me: the fringed gill-arches and movable operculum; the pores of the head, fleshly lips, and lidless eyes; the lateral line, the spinous fins, and forked tail; the compressed and arched body. When I had finished, he waited as if expecting more, and then, with an air of disappointment,—

"You have not looked very carefully; why," he continued, more earnestly, "you haven't even seen one of the most conspicuous features of the animal, which is as plainly before your eyes as the fish itself; look again, look again!" and he left me to my misery.

I was piqued; I was mortified. Still more of that wretched fish? But now I set myself to my task with a will, and discovered one new thing after another, until I saw how just the professor's criticism had been. The afternoon passed quickly, and when, toward its close, the professor inquired,—

"Do you see it yet?"

"No," I replied, "I am certain I do not, but I see how little I saw before."

"That is next best," said he, earnestly, "but I won't hear you now; put away your fish and go home; perhaps you will be ready with a better answer in the morning. I will examine you before you look at the fish."

This was disconcerting; not only must I think of my fish all night, studying, without the object before me, what this unknown but most visible feature might be, but also, without reviewing my new discoveries, I must give an exact account of them the next day. I had a bad memory; so I walked home by Charles River in a distracted state, with my two perplexities.

The cordial greeting from the professor the next morning was reassuring; here was a man who seemed to be quite as anxious as I, that I should see for myself what he saw.

"Do you perhaps mean," I asked, "that the fish has symmetrical sides with paired organs?"

His thoroughly pleased, "Of course, of course!" repaid the wakeful hours of the previous night. After he had discoursed most happily and enthusiastically—as he always did—upon the importance of this point, I ventured to ask what I should do next.

"Oh, look at your fish!" he said, and left me again to my own devices. In a little more than an hour he returned and heard my new catalogue.

"That is good, that is good!" he repeated; "but that is not all; go on;" and so for three long days he placed that fish before my eyes, forbidding me to look at anything else, or to use any artificial aid. "Look, look, look," was his repeated injunction.

This was the best entomological lesson I ever had,—a lesson whose influence has extended to the details of every subsequent study; a legacy the professor has left to me, as he left it to many others, of inestimable value, which we could not buy, with which we cannot part.

A year afterwards, some of us were amusing ourselves with chalking outlandish beasts upon the museum blackboard. We drew prancing starfishes; frogs in mortal combat; hydra-headed worms; stately crawfishes, standing on their tails, bearing aloft umbrellas; and grotesque fishes with gaping mouths and staring eyes. The professor came in shortly after, and was as amused as any at our experiments. He looked at the fishes.

"Hæmulons, every one of them," he said; "Mr.---- drew them."

True; and to this day, if I attempt a fish, I can draw nothing but Hæmulons.

The fourth day, a second fish of the same group was placed beside the first, and I was bidden to point out the resemblances and differences between the two; another and another followed, until the entire family lay before me, and a whole legion of jars covered the table and surrounding shelves; the odor had become a pleasant perfume: and even now, the sight of an old, six-inch, worm-eaten cork brings fragrant memories!

The whole group of Hæmulons was thus brought in review: and, whether engaged upon the dissection of the internal organs, the preparation and examination of the bony frame-work, or the description of the various parts, Agassiz's training in the method of observing facts and their orderly arrangement was ever accompanied by the urgent exhortation not to be content with them.

"Facts are stupid things," he would say, "until brought into connection with some general law."

At the end of eight months, it was almost with reluctance that I left these friends and turned to insects: but what I had gained by this outside experience has been of greater value than years of later investigation in my favorite groups.

QUESTIONS FOR FURTHER THOUGHT

Discussion Questions:

1. How did the professor relate to the student?
2. What did the professor keep telling the student?
3. What "methods" of teaching did the professor use?
4. What did the professor have to say about a pencil?
5. How long did it take the student to see all that could be seen?
6. Who asked the most questions? What kinds of questions were there?
7. In what way was the professor as eager as the student?
8. What was the motivation of the student? Was the student competing against anyone?
9. What happened a year after the student had experienced the class?

Interpretation Questions:

1. What is this story communicating?
2. Why did the professor not use books about fish? Explain the difference between primary sources and secondary sources?
3. What does the following statement mean—"Facts are stupid things . . . until brought into connection with some general law"? Do you agree or disagree? Why?

Application Questions:

1. What relationship does this story have with Bible study?
2. What principle can you take from this story into your personal Bible study?
3. From the responses to the two previous questions and from the story, summarize all the application statements that apply to Bible study.

Additional Activities:

1. Draw a picture of the student looking at a fish.
2. Use the color yellow and color the lines in the story that tell us the instructions and directions the professor gave to the student.
3. Use the color orange and underline the places in the story that tell you how the student was feeling. What do you see? Have you ever felt this way? Explain when you did.

CHAPTER TWO

PREREQUISITES OF BIBLE STUDY

God has equipped each of us to study the Bible since He has given us two ears to hear and two eyes to see. The tasks in Bible study are listening with our ears and reading with our eyes.

LISTENING

God made us with one mouth and two ears. In creating us this way, what do you think He was saying? Might it infer (as some wise person may have told you) that we need to listen twice as much as we talk? Or is it simply aesthetically more pleasing? We all know that listening is important, but we do not always choose to do it. Luke 8:1-18 contains the parable of the soil. A more accurate title is the "Parable of the Ears." All heard, but the response to what they heard is most significant. Sometimes Jesus speaks to the general populace in confusing stories. Notice, the disciples are the ones who desire to know the story's meaning. Jesus tells them the meaning. Are we to have such a desire to listen before we can understand? Yes! Jesus showed grace to the people since their understanding was minimal and they were uninterested in pursuing His meaning. Because they did not seek understanding, their judgment would be less severe than if they had understood what Jesus was saying. Jesus holds people accountable for what they understand. If we listen and desire understanding, then actions must follow. By listening, more content is imparted, giving the listener responsibility! The desire to listen is critical! If such a desire is not present, then what we hear will not take root. The listening process is a progression: listening leads to understanding that leads to godly behavior. If we hear and understand, then the Teacher gives us more. Students who listen and respond receive more. If one carefully listens, more is heard. Therefore, listening is one of the keys to the inner treasures of the soul.

Scripture has much to say about listening. Proverbs particularly speaks of the benefits of listening (2:1-5; 15:31; 21:13; 23:12; 28:9). Listening is a spiritual discipline. By listening, we give control to the person who is talking and communicate their worth to them. We communicate the desire to understand and to take seriously what the person has to say, we grow in our relationships, and we reveal our inner self and communicate worth to the speaker. Our open ears reveal responsive hearts. If we cannot listen to others, how well will we listen to God?[3]

One way to listen is to read the Bible and hear what God has said. When reading the Bible, ask yourself the question, "Am I listening to what God has said?" The first task to serious Bible study is listening—listening to the Word of God.

Learn to listen to God before speaking for God.

READING THE BIBLE[4]

Followers of Christ are often encouraged to read the Bible—and for good reasons. One reason is to understand what God is saying now and what He has said in the past. This kind of Bible reading is a utilitarian approach. We read to know what directions to follow in life. This is often our purpose when we read the Bible silently, but there is also a place for reading the Bible aloud. Prior to the printing press and the proliferation of technology, people read the Bible out loud.

What is the benefit of reading the Bible aloud? First, we read slower. We see the printed word. We hear the printed word. When we see and hear the Word, more of our senses are activated, more energy goes into the text and life is breathed into the words on the page. Public reading of the Word seems to have diminished over the years, yet the Bible gives clear direction in the importance of the reading of God's Word.

3. R. Banks and R. P. Stevens. *The Complete Book of Everyday Christianity*, "Listening," (Downers Grove, IL: InterVarsity Press), 588-590.
4. A classic book on the topic of reading is *How To Read a Book* by Mortimer Adler and Mark Van Doren. They give four levels of reading—(1) "Elementary" or basic reading, (2) "Inspectional" reading, (3) "Analytical" reading with the purpose of understanding the text, and (4) "Comparative" reading where one book is compared to another.

How often do you hear God's Word read in public? Is the Word read aloud in your church meeting each Sunday? Do you read the Word aloud? Usually, the Bible is read silently. However, Deuteronomy 17:14-20 speaks of the importance of the king's writing out the law each day so that the Word is with him and so that he will read the word aloud, revere it and obey it. Deuteronomy 11:16-21 also speaks of the importance of the public reading of God's Word.

Historically, people read aloud so others could hear and understand since books were not plentiful. Such an example is found in Acts 8:26-40, the account of Philip who hears the reading of the Word and asks if understanding is occurring. Thus, the auditory reading of the Word opened a seeking heart for reconciliation. Revelation 1:3 says that those who read the words of its prophecy are blessed!

Bible reading in the early church was called *lectio divina*, a special and unique way of reading in that it was slow and reflective with the desire to be touched and transformed by God. It is not hurried; it is quality rather than quantity reading. Divine reading "is a way of reading for formation and transformation, not for information ... Read the passage of Scripture aloud. Listen to the sound of each word. Read slowly, and rest as you listen. Remember—this is a time to listen, not to dissect, analyze, evaluate or dialogue."[5]

TYPES OF CREATIVE READING

Hearing Scripture read aloud—publicly or privately—incorporates more than one sense and thereby can increase understanding. The following are some ideas to help make the public reading of the Word meaningful.

1. **Unison reading.** The entire group reads the passage together with unified expression and word inflections. E.g. Jeremiah 5:21-29.
2. **Responsive reading.** A leader reads a portion, and then the entire group reads a portion in response. This may be done many times. E.g. Psalm 136:1-9.
3. **Emphasis reading.** The passage is read with various readers emphasizing key concepts in the passage, e.g. a repeated word, etc.; or one group reads a verse and a second group repeats two to four important words in the verse. E.g. John 1:1-8.

5. Jan Ord. "Listening for the Whisper of the Beloved," *Union Life*, Sept/Oct 1998, pp. 20-21.

4. **Dramatic or Script reading.** This requires a historical or narrative passage with various people so readers read their lines with a narrator reading what is in between. E.g. Genesis 22:1-19; Matthew 4:1-11; Mark 4:35-42.

5. **Character reading.** A person reads what a character says in a long passage of scripture, e.g. Jesus' prayer in John 17. It is important for the character to be introduced prior to his/her reading. E.g. Numbers 22:21-35.

6. **Antiphonal reading.** Two or three groups of people read various verses or parts of verses as if responding from one to the other. E.g. Psalm 150.

7. **Monologue reading.** One person reads with good enunciation and dynamic expression. E.g. Psalm 13.

8. **Choral reading.** Different group sizes (i.e. solos, duets, trios, whole groups, etc.) read verses together. E.g. Daniel 7:1-10; Isaiah 35:1-10.

9. **Read and explain.** A verse is read and then someone paraphrases it or briefly explains what it means. E.g. Psalm 121.

10. **Read with sound effects.** Read a passage as someone else provides appropriate sound effects. (Of course, the passage must support these sounds!) E.g. Jonah 1; Mark 4:35-42.

BENEFITS OF READING

What are the benefits of reading the text? Many, but here are a few:

1. An overview of the passage, chapter, or book.
2. Major impressions are formed within the mind of the reader.
3. A feel for the flow of the passage, chapter, or book.
4. General facts within the passage, chapter, or book.
5. Knowledge of the plot or argument of the passage, chapter, or book.
6. A taste of the genre of the passage, chapter, or book.

A READER'S PRAYER

Reading begins the process of God's opening our spiritual eyes. It leads to understanding and proceeds to Bible study. Many Christians just read the Bible and never move to the next step—study. Before study can take place, reading must occur. Those who stop at the reading level usually read the Bible to see and understand the perspective found in the Bible (macroscopic reading). However, study begins when the student picks up a pencil/pen/keyboard and begins to interact with the text. At this point, reading becomes more detailed (microscopic). Reading is the first step, but not the last!

> Leave me not, O gracious Presence, in such hours as I may today devote to the reading of books or of newspapers. Guide my mind to choose the right books and, having chosen them, to read them in the right way. When I read for profit, grant that all I read may lead me nearer to thyself. When I read for recreation, grant that what I read may not lead me away from thee. Let all my reading refresh my mind that I may more eagerly seek after whatsoever things are pure and fair and true.
>
> *John Baillie*[6]

EXERCISE

Read Luke 8:1-15 slowly, carefully, and aloud, then reflect on the passage in light of this chapter's content.

---

6. James W. Sire. *Habits of the Mind.* (Downer's Grove, IL: InterVarsity Press), 177.

CHAPTER THREE
BASICS OF BIBLE STUDY

TWO APPROACHES TO BIBLE STUDY

Consider a medical doctor. She illustrates the inductive approach by studying a patient's problem on the basis of a thorough evaluation of all the factors involved. She studies the whole person by asking many questions—medical history, diet, exercise and habits. She takes blood tests or x-rays. After studying the facts, she inductively draws a conclusion about diagnosis and treatment. These conclusions are tentative since she is always open to further questions and new observations as she grows in her understanding of the patient and his problem. This is an example of the inductive process.

On the other hand, deductive Bible study is approaching the Scriptures with the expressed purpose of proving a particular predetermined concept or idea. Instead of being motivated by openness to the Lord and the resulting freedom to ask questions of the Scripture, one is motivated to understand a passage from only one perspective. This type of study often results in error since only the Scriptures which support that concept or idea are used.

A lawyer illustrates the deductive approach by the way he develops a case to defend his client in a court of law. His client comes to him explaining all the factors in the allegation. The lawyer then picks and chooses the aspects of his client's story that can corroborate and be effectively defended in court. All parts of the story that are not helpful in building a winning case are discarded or diminished.

OVERVIEW OF THE INGREDIENTS OF BIBLE STUDY

Bible study is a process that requires a proper attitude. The student's attitude is to be one of humility, asking God to reveal what His Word says. This is an attitude that God creates in the heart and life of the student, as she is open to Him. It is an attitude of openness to God's teaching that frees the student to ask questions of the Scripture instead of being confined to search for proof of a pre-determined idea.

All Bible study begins with the reading of the Word. Often this is where most believers stop, but there is much more. Reading from various translations and paraphrases can be most helpful; however, reading should lead to the study of the Word. As previously stated, there are many benefits to reading the Bible, but reading is just the beginning of the study process!

There are seven essential ingredients for Bible study. Generally, these ingredients do not have a specific order, for at times they are interchanged, rearranged, and even overlap. However, the observation, interpretation, application sequence **must** occur in that order. There are seven ingredients for interactive Bible study: 1) Prayer, 2) Historical Background, 3) Observation—Seeing, 4) Interpretation—Understanding, 5) Application—Responding, 6) Synthesis or Summarization, and 7) Correlation.

Observation, **interpretation** and **application** go together. Observation is seeing the Word as recorded in the book being studied. **Observation** is responding to the question, "What do I see?" This is a fact-finding question. Record the significant facts that answer the questions. Because you are looking at the various parts of a passage in a systematic way, you are enabled to see that portion from a deeper perspective. As you have prayed, God will open eyes!

> Open my eyes that I may see wonderful things in your law.
>
> Psalms 119:18

Interpretation is seeking the meaning as the Holy Spirit opens heart and eyes. **Interpretation** is "What did it mean to the original audience? What does it mean to me?" This is the work of the Holy Spirit, interacting with the student's mind and thought processes. Sometimes interpretation immediately results in action, just as turning on the light switch brings light to a room. At other times, interpretation is like a light with a dimmer switch. The brilliance of the light slowly comes. Interpretation may be a process that leads to asking additional questions of the text that require further study. Always ask yourself: "What do my observations lead me to understand?" Interpretation is not necessarily one single act, but is often the process and discipline of meditation. Paul told

Timothy to "Be diligent (King James' translation used the word "meditate") in these matters; give yourself wholly to them. . . ." (1 Timothy 4:15). The process of interpretation is also helped by the correlation and summarization elements of Bible study, which are explained later. Jeremiah gives an example of this observation-interpretation dynamic.

> The word of the LORD came to me: "What do you see, Jeremiah?" "I see the branch of an almond tree," I replied. The LORD said to me, "You have seen correctly, for I am watching to see that my word is fulfilled." The word of the LORD came to me again: "What do you see?" "I see a boiling pot, tilting away from the north," I answered. The LORD said to me, "From the north disaster will be poured out on all who live in the land. I am about to summon all the peoples of the northern kingdoms," declares the LORD. "Their kings will come and set up their thrones in the entrance of the gates of Jerusalem; they will come against all her surrounding walls and against all the towns of Judah.
>
> Jeremiah 1:11-15

Application is asking the question, "What does it mean to me?" As God reveals Himself through His Word, He applies the Scripture to your own personal life situation. Always ask yourself: "What do my observations and insights mean to me personally? What is God saying to me through my study? Now that I know this truth, what I am going to do about it?" **Application** is bringing the interpretation to reality in our lives.

> Anyone who listens to the word but does not do what it says is like a man who looks at his face in a mirror and, after looking at himself, goes away and immediately forgets what he looks like. But the man who looks intently into the perfect law that gives freedom, and continues to do this, not forgetting what he has heard, but doing it he will be blessed in what he does.
>
> James 1:23-25

In this method of Bible study, **synthesis** is taking certain observations and facts and charting them together. **Synthesis** is like the table of contents interlaced with the index of a book, giving a big picture with some of the essential concepts of the book. This gives us a picture of the flow, the development and the relationships that connect the major themes to each other.

However, I consider my life worth nothing to me, if only I may finish the race and complete the task the Lord Jesus has given me—the task of testifying to the gospel of God's grace. "Now I know that none of you among whom I have gone about preaching the kingdom will ever see me again. Therefore, I declare to you today that I am innocent of the blood of all men. For I have not hesitated to proclaim to you the whole will of God."

Acts 20:24-27

In this method of Bible study, **correlation** is taking other Scripture passages, studying them, and then observing relationships between these Scriptures. Often these relationships bring greater clarity to each of the Scriptures. When I took college English Literature, our professor urged us to discover the spiritual gems in the text—associating Scriptures with Chaucer or other writers. I believe God desires us to bring Scriptural connections to song lyrics, books, stories, movies, and life experiences. **Correlation** in Bible study is an on-going building process, not connecting verses to verses but passages to passages, paragraphs to paragraphs, chapters to books. Correlation increases understanding so that application can be clearly defined and produced.

Now that same day two of them were going to a village called Emmaus, about seven miles from Jerusalem. . . And beginning with Moses and all the Prophets, he explained to them what was said in all the Scriptures concerning himself. . . He said to them, "This is what I told you while I was still with you: Everything must be fulfilled that is written about me in the Law of Moses, the Prophets and the Psalms." Then he opened their minds so they could understand the Scriptures.

Luke 24:13, 27, 44, 45

APPLICATION EXERCISE

Now that Bible Study is explained, begin your study journey by reading Psalm 1 five times in its entirety. Read from different versions of the Bible.

PRAYER, THE CONTINUOUS PROCESS

Prayer is acknowledging that God is the One who must reveal Himself to us. We cannot know God by means of our own mind or discipline. Without the ministry of the Holy Spirit, we walk in darkness, stumbling over the toys and blocks placed in our path by Satan or our sinful selves. Prayer is acknowledging our desperate need for Him to be the light to our path. When Jesus speaks about the ministry of the Holy Spirit in John 14-16, He teaches us (you and me) a truth that lifts us up. God teaches me what I need to know as He opens my eyes to Himself and His reality in the worlds in which I function.

> But when he, the Spirit of truth, comes, he will guide you into all truth. He will not speak on his own; he will speak only what he hears, and he will tell you what is yet to come.
>
> John 16:13

Psalm 119 is filled with the psalmist's pleas to open his mind and heart to realize and experience the amazing God that He is (Psalm 119:18). The request to teach the psalmist to obey and to give him understanding is repeated numerous times. Ask God to open your mind to understand the truth of the Word. Prayer is not just before one begins to study, but it continues throughout study. To study the Bible without prayer is like trying to bathe without water.

HISTORICAL BACKGROUND

Learning the historical background helps create the context in which the author and recipients lived. Often as questions arise during study, one will have to seek further historical information. Use your own Bible and a good Bible handbook or history resource for this important information.

> Many have undertaken to draw up an account of the things that have been fulfilled among us, just as they were handed down to us by those who from the first were eyewitnesses and servants of the word. Therefore, since I myself have carefully investigated everything from the beginning, it seemed good also to me to write an orderly account for you, most excellent Theophilus, so that you may know the certainty of the things you have been taught.
>
> Luke 1:1-4

The goal of studying historical background is to understand the historical context in which the book was written and experienced. If you were to ask one of your parents, or a friend, to examine their love letters, (and if they would permit you to do this), would you be able to understand what is being said? Possibly you would understand some of what they had written, but greater comprehension would come by asking questions like, "Where were you at this time in your life?" or "What did you mean by this statement?" By asking the question to the author, you are able to grasp the context of the letter. We must come to God's Word in the same way! Historical background is like looking at the envelope when you are returning from the mailbox. The envelope informs you of several important things: 1) who this letter is to, 2) who this letter is from, 3) the date the letter was sent, 4) the place from which it was sent, and 5) the method by which it arrived at your home (usually by a mail carrier!). This "envelope idea" is applicable to every book of the Bible; however, all the "envelopes" have been lost so we must look at the letter/book itself to discover what the envelope would have told us. Various books of the Bible will respond differently to these questions; sometimes the answers are clear, and sometimes ambiguous, at which point we must go outside the Bible itself to find some helpful answers from other historical sources.

To summarize, we want to build the historical context of the book of the Bible by uncovering the following:

1. **Author**. Who wrote the book?
2. **Recipients**. To whom was the book written?
3. **Location**. From where was the book written?
4. **Date**. When was the book written?
5. **Purpose**. What is the book's purpose?

In gathering historical background material, first look at the book itself, asking the question, "What does this book tell me about the author, recipients, location, date, and purpose?" If the question is not answered, enlarge your search to the entire Bible, asking the question, "What does the BIBLE tell me about the author, etc.?" The information that is found is labeled "Internal Evidence" because the book or the Bible gives us the answer. However, if some of the questions are not answered, then we must turn to "External Evidence." This means that information from sources other than the Bible is needed. This is usually found in Bible reference tools, such as Bible dictionaries, Bible handbooks, atlases, concordances, and books on Bible customs. Chapter 4 gives a list of some helpful reference tools. Examples of a basic historical background worksheet are on the following pages. Remember to apply what you learned from Bible study tools to the passage you are working with.

WORKSHEET

HISTORICAL BACKGROUND BASIC

INTERNAL EVIDENCE *Primary Source with Reference*	EXTERNAL EVIDENCE *Secondary Sources**
1. Author. Who wrote the book?	
2. Recipients. To whom was this book written?	
3. Location. From where was the book written?	
4. Date. When was the book written?	
5. Purpose. Why was the book written	

* Be sure to document your sources.

WORSHEET

HISTORICAL BACKGROUND: EXAMPLE ON OBADIAH

INTERNAL EVIDENCE *Primary Source with Reference*	EXTERNAL EVIDENCE *Secondary Sources**
1. Author. Who wrote the book? 1:1 Obadiah's vision (Authorship not specifically stated though inferred in verse one.)	Obadiah means "Worshipper of Yahweh/God" or "Servant of Yahweh" (Blankenbaker, 185) Nothing is known about the writer's background; 12 Obadiahs in the OT according to *Zondervan Pictorial Bible Dictionary*, page 592.
2. Recipients. To whom was this book written? 1:1 vision about Edom or Edomites who were descendants of Esau	Edom was a long-time enemy of Judah. The Herods were Edomites. Edom had previous contact with the nation of Judah. (*Eerdman's Handbook to the Bible*, 447)
3. Location. From where was the book written? Location is not stated though Edom is stated in 1:1. Other locations noted: Jerusalem, Mount Zion, Negev, Canaan, Zarephath, Sepharad, Teman, Halah	Edom — a name derived from the Semitic root meaning 'red,' 'ruddy' and given to the area situated south of the Dead Sea on both sides of the Wadi Arabah because of the reddish color of the sandstone of that district. (*Harper's Bible Dictionary*, page 246, Logos software)
4. Date. When was the book written? Text does not say.	Disputed dates that offer 3 options: (1) 848-841 BC; (2) 731-715 BC; (3) 586 BC — #1 and #3 are most popular with conservative scholars. (Archer, 287) What other events were occurring at this time? Babylonians attacked Judah. Edomites were happy about this, helping Babylonian army. They looted Jerusalem, as well as helped the Babylonians catch fleeing Jews. In 581 BC Nebuchadnezzar drove Edomites from their rocky home. Years later, the Edomites completely disappeared from history. (*What the Bible Is All About for Young Explorers*, p. 185)
5. Purpose. Why was the book written? Purpose is not clearly stated although v. 10 states the reason for the vision in that Edom will be destroyed since they did not come to the rescue of their brother Jacob. v. 10 To inform Edom of coming destruction—"Because of the violence against your brother Jacob . . you will be destroyed."	

* SOURCES

- Achtemier, Paul J.(editor) *Harper's Bible Dictionary.* New York: Harper and Row, 1973.
- Alexander, David and Pat. *Eerdmans' Handbook to the Bible.* Grand Rapids, MI: Eerdmans Publishing Company, 1978.
- Archer, Gleason. *A Survey of Old Testament Introduction.* Chicago, IL: Moody Press, 1973.
- Blankenbaker, Frances. *What the Bible is All About for Young Explorers.* Venture, CA: Regal Books, 1986.
- Tenney, Merrill C. (editor) The *Zondervan Pictorial Bible Dictionary.* Grand Rapids, MI: Zondervan Publishing House, 1978.

OBSERVATION EXERCISES

Interactive Bible study involves making clear and accurate observations. There can be numerous observation exercises. The following two observation exercises are basic in discovering some of the riches in God's Word.

OBSERVATION EXERCISE #1: TWO TECHNIQUES

Observation #1 is the fact sheet for recording and organizing observations. Your ability to observe will develop as you learn to ask basic questions, the answers to which are found in the Scriptures you are studying. Remember to answer the questions on the bases of paragraphs, each of which usually contains one central thought. Since most Bibles divide the text into paragraphs, you can use their paragraph designations.

TECHNIQUE #1: ESSENCE

As you study a section of Scripture, take one paragraph at a time and write the answers to the questions on your worksheet. This exercise asks three core questions:

1. **Who are the characters? What are they doing? (Left or first column)**

   People, subjects, and/or concepts that are doing or saying something are considered characters—the who of the paragraph. Of course, this could also be the "what" of the paragraph. Begin with the first paragraph, read through the text, and then record each respective person or thing. Next, briefly describe what is being done or said by them in the paragraph. Use the text. Sometimes the sentences may be long, but look for the main idea. In one sense, this column is identifying the subjects or nouns accompanied by the predicates, or more specifically, the verbs. Record the subject and verb, deleting prepositional phrases, conjunctions, adverbs and adjectives—words that elaborate on the main idea. These observations are recorded in the first column. An example is found on page 30.

2. **What is the main idea? What is the main point of the paragraph? (Middle)**

   The main idea of the paragraph expresses the basic truth of the paragraph by summarizing its contents in five words or less—making a title. Possibly a quotation or a summary from the paragraph itself could be used as the title. In light of what you have written in the left column, ask yourself this question, "What is the author saying?" The main idea must be supported by all the other ideas in the paragraph. It is like a wheel, with the hub being the main idea and the spokes being the supporting facts. You will later use this main idea as a title for the paragraph. Please keep it to five words or less. This will encourage you to choose concise words!

3. Why is this important? What is the significance of the main idea? (Right)

The third column is answering the "why" question. The following questions are beneficial: "If this paragraph was absent from the scriptures, what important things would be missing? What things—action, attitudes, descriptions—would I not know?" These questions attempt to walk in the author's shoes by seeking the motivation of the action. In comparison to the previous two questions, this question is more subjective; however, stay as close to the text as possible since the author will usually suggest the reason for its worth. At times, it may be better to move to the next paragraph if you are having difficulty making this observation. (See page 30 for an example.)

TECHNIQUE #2: STRUCTURAL ANALYSIS

The structural model is a way of displaying every word of the Scripture text so that interconnections between the grammatical parts become clear. A structural model does not rephrase the text nor delete any of the text; it merely breaks it up and indents it onto separate lines to highlight the connections and the structure of the passage. The purpose of the structural model is to fit the passage together, recognize interpretive problems and begin to develop an understanding of the passage's flow of thought. The structural model is not the same thing as the interpretation step in Bible study. It is one way to observe the Scriptural passage. In recording observations using this approach, follow these general guidelines in the first column of your worksheet::

- Divide the passage into logical divisions and then work one passage at a time. Usually your Bible has divided the passage into paragraphs; use the structure given.
- Start with the main (independent) sentences or commands at the left margin. Distinguish main statements from explanations.
- Place any dependent phrases or clauses under the words they modify.
- Make parallel phrases obvious. If necessary, connect them with lines.
- Place lists of qualities, actions, etc., in a vertical column.
- Identify the repeated words of the text by highlighting them in **bold** or the color green. (These crucial words are candidates for word studies.)
- Let the structure reveal the big idea of the text.

Note: There is no "right" or "wrong" way to display a structural model; however, it must represent your efforts to understand the passage and its logical connections. The middle and right columns are completed as for ESSENCE. An example is given on page 31.

WORKSHEET

PHILIPPIANS 1:1-18B

An Example of Observation #1 using the Essence Approach

WHO / WHAT	MAIN IDEA / TITLE	WHY / SIGNIFICANCE
Paul Timothy Saints in Christ Jesus Overseers Deacons God our Father (grace and peace from) Lord Jesus Christ	1:1-2 "Paul to Philippians: Grace and Peace"	• Identifies the author and the recipients • Gives descriptions of each • States who our source of grace and peace is—God the Father!!

I (Paul) ...
    thank God
    remember you
    always pray
    have you
    am in chains
    long for you
You (Philippians) ...
    are partners
    share in God's grace
may discern, be pure and filled
God ...
    began a good work
    will carry it out
    can testify
	1:3-11
	
	"Prayer: Thanks God for Partners"
	
	or
	
	"Paul's Joyful Prayer of Thanksgiving"
		• Tells how Paul is praying
		• See the expression of many feelings
		• God began a good work

I (Paul)
    want you to know
    am put here
    am in chains
Brothers in the Lord
    have been encouraged
    preach Christ
    stir up trouble
Others
    will preach Christ
Christ
    is preached
	1:12-18b
	
	"Motives of the Preachers of the Gospel"
		• How the gospel has been advanced through Paul's bondage
		• Paul's response to negative motives for preaching
		• Paul's purpose of "why am I here?"
		• Preaching motives are contrasted

PHILIPPIANS 1:1-18B

An Example of Observation #1 using the Structural Analysis Approach

STRUCTURAL ANALYSIS	MAIN IDEA / TITLE	WHY / SIGNIFICANCE

Paul and Timothy,
      servants of Christ Jesus,
To all the saints
      in Christ Jesus at Philippi,
together with the overseers and deacons:
² Grace and peace to you
      from God our Father and
      the Lord Jesus Christ.
	1:1-2
	
	"Paul to Philippians:
	Grace and Peace"
		• Identifies the author and the recipients
		• Gives descriptions of each
		• States who our source of grace and peace is—God the Father!!

I thank my God every time
I remember you.
    in all my prayers for all of you,
I always pray with joy
    because of your partnership
      in the gospel
from the first day until now,
being confident of this, that he who
    began a good work in you
will carry it on to completion
until the day of Christ Jesus.
It is right for me to feel this way
    about all of you, since
I have you in my heart;
      for whether
I am in chains or defending and
    confirming the gospel,
all of you share in God's grace with me.
⁸ God can testify how I long for all of you
with the affection of Christ Jesus. And
this is my prayer:
that your love may abound more and
    more in knowledge and
    depth of insight,
    so that
you may be able to discern
what is best and
may be pure and
blameless
until the day of Christ,
filled with the fruit of righteousness that
comes through Jesus Christ—
to the glory and praise of God.
	1:3-11
	
	"Prayer: Thanks God
	for Partners"
	
	or
	
	"Paul's Joyful Prayer
	of Thanksgiving"
		• Tells how Paul is praying
		• See the expression of many feelings
		• God began a good work

OBSERVATION EXERCISES

OBSERVATION EXERCISE #2

This second observation exercise further develops visual skills by discovering the six basic forms of expression found throughout Scripture and literature. We all use these forms to one extent or another. If a friend said that you look like your mother, father, or sibling, a form of expression was used! God's Word will take on more significance as you observe the specific forms an author uses to convey his ideas, thoughts and experiences.

Forms of expression can often be found by crucial terms that link the ideas together. These are key words, as they will often identify the expression. However, once these words are found, be sure they identify a form of expression because, at times, they are used as other parts of speech, such as conjunctions. Also, many of the major forms of expression contain no connective words. The questions to ask are, "What kind of expression is this?" and "What makes it so?"

For the purpose of observation, it is very helpful to have a consistent color code as you mark these forms of expression. A suggested color code is given, but you may adapt and change the code to fit your style.

EXPLANATION OF THE FORMS OF EXPRESSION

1. **Comparisons:** This is the author's way of describing an object or idea by comparing it with something similar or by giving an illustration.

    Key Connectives: LIKE, AS, JUST AS, SUCH AS

    Color Code: BLACK

    Examples: "You look just like your mother."

    Psalm 1:3a — "He is like a tree planted by streams of water . . . . "

2. **Contrasts:** Authors use contrast—the association of opposites—as a means of emphasizing or clarifying a point. When the connective word is observed, the question that arises is, "What opposite is found here?"

    Key Connectives: BUT, YET, RATHER THAN, HOWEVER

    Color Code: RED

    Example: Mother wants her coffee hot but I want it cold.

    Psalm 1:6 (NIV) – For the LORD watches over the way of the righteous, but the way of the wicked will perish." Way of the righteousness is contrasted with the way of the wicked.

3. **Repetition:** In order to emphasize a point, a writer repeats words, phrases, or ideas. These repetitions are important.

    No key connectives: look for WORDS, PHRASES, CONCEPTS, and IDEAS

    (Note: As you study the Word, you will soon be able to pick out words that are important. For example, the word "righteousness" is a frequent word and usually is an important word in passages where it is repeated.)

    Color Code: GREEN

    Example: "Yes, yes, yes, by all means go for it!"

    Psalm 1:4-6 — "Not so the wicked! They are like chaff that the wind blows away. Therefore the wicked will not stand in the judgment, nor sinners in the assembly of the righteous. For the LORD watches over the way of the righteous, but the way of the wicked will perish." Repetition of the "wicked" and the concept of evil is seen in these verses.

4. **Cause and Effect:** In order to explain and clarify an idea or condition, an author may describe what caused the condition and what resulted from it. At times the author will reverse the order and state the cause first.

    Key Connectives: BECAUSE, FOR - often introduces a reason

    SO THAT — sets forth a purpose

    THEREFORE — may state a result or conclusion, often introduces a summary of ideas

    IF ... THEN — sets forth a cause which will bring certain results

    IF, IF SO — calls for action, a condition

    Color Code: ORANGE

    Examples: "If you will do this for me, then I will do the other for you."

    John 5:39a, "You diligently study the Scriptures because you think that by them you possess eternal life." Because you think Scriptures have eternal life, the effect is that you study them.

5. **Progression and lists:** An author may give a list or series of ideas or items. There are reasons for lists and the order of the lists in Scripture. By using several steps, the author can show a movement to a particular result. So, in a progression, each step builds on the one before it. Progressions can be indicated by placing an arrow in the margin with the tip of the arrow pointing in the direction of the progression. You may find it helpful to write the steps of the progression in the margin

along with the arrow, or to place numbers within the text designating the sequence.

No key connectives, give the list or progression a title.

Color Code: BLUE

Example: "When you go to the grocery store, please get me some hamburgers, buns, ketchup ..."

Psalm 1:1 — "Blessed is the man who does not walk in the counsel of the wicked or stand in the way of sinners or sit in the seat of mockers." Here the progression of walk, stand, sit is stated with movement from proceeding in a certain direction to sitting down with no progress made in arriving at the final destination.

6. **Summary Statements:** This is a concise statement that ties together all that has been said before or after the statement. It is usually an all-inclusive statement. Often after a concept has been discussed, it is summarized in one succinct sentence, or possibly in a phrase.

Key Connectives: THEREFORE (sometimes), IN SUMMARY

Color Code: BROWN

Example: "Tell me about your day." Stating the general happenings or an event that was positive or negative usually summarizes this request.

1 Peter 4:19 — "So then, those who suffer according to God's will should commit themselves to their faithful Creator and continue to do good." This summarizes 4:12-18 in one sentence.

EXERCISE

Use Psalm 1 and identify as many forms of expression as you can. Psalm 1 is packed with them! Use colors because it increases visual perception and identification.

[1]Blessed is the man who does not walk in the counsel of the wicked or stand in the way of sinners or sit in the seat of mockers.

[2]But his delight is in the law of the LORD, and on his law he meditates day and night.

[3]He is like a tree planted by streams of water, which yields its fruit in season and whose leaf does not wither. Whatever he does prospers.

[4]Not so the wicked! They are like chaff that the wind blows away.

[5]Therefore the wicked will not stand in the judgment, nor sinners in the assembly of the righteous.

[6]For the LORD watches over the way of the righteous, but the way of the wicked will perish.

VALID OBSERVATIONS LEAD TO INTERPRETATION AND APPLICATION

The following page is an example of Observation Exercise #2.

OBSERVATION EXERCISE

JONAH 1:1-12

CONTRAST

¹The word of the LORD came to Jonah son of Amittai: ²"Go to the great city of Nineveh and preach against it, **because** its wickedness has come up before me." ³**But** Jonah ran away from the LORD and headed for Tarshish. He went down to Joppa, where he found a ship bound for that port. After paying the fare, he went aboard and sailed for Tarshish to flee from the LORD.

CAUSE & EFFECT   **REPETITION OF A CONCEPT**

⁴Then the LORD sent a great wind on the sea, and such a violent storm arose that the ship threatened to break up. ⁵All the sailors were afraid and each cried out to his own god. And they threw the cargo into the sea to lighten the ship. **But** Jonah had gone below deck, where he lay down and fell into a deep sleep. ⁶The captain went to him and said, "How can you sleep? Get up and call on your god! Maybe he will take notice of us, and we will not perish." ⁷Then the sailors said to each other, "Come, let us cast lots to find out who is responsible for this calamity." They cast lots and the lot fell on Jonah. ⁸So they asked him, "Tell us, who is responsible for making all this trouble for us? What do you do? Where do you come from? What is your country? From what people are you?" ⁹He answered, "I am a Hebrew and I worship the LORD, the God of heaven, who made the sea and the land."

REPETITION OF QUESTIONS   **CONTRAST BETWEEN ACTION OF SAILORS AND JONAH**

¹⁰This terrified them and they asked, "What have you done?" (They knew he was running away from the LORD, **because** he had already told them so.) ¹¹The sea was getting rougher and rougher. So they asked him, "What should we do to you to make the sea calm down for us?" ¹²"Pick me up and throw me into the sea," he replied, "and it will become calm. I know that it is my fault that this great storm has come upon you."

CAUSE & EFFECT

OBSERVATIONS

No summary sentences in these verses—this is a story!

Since Jonah is a story, it is a continuous progression although there are short and concise progressions that may be identified, e.g. in verse 3:

1. went to Joppa
2. found a ship
3. paid the fare
4. went aboard
5. sailed for Tarshish

Title: Jonah's Expedient Departure

Note: *Color-coding makes observations much easier to see.*

INTERPRETATION AND UNDERSTANDING

Good, reliable, and valid observations lead to correct understanding. God does not play hide-'n-seek with us. God desires to reveal Himself to us. His Word speaks to us today as we listen, desire to understand, and obey the spoken Word. As we understand the narrative in its time period and the truth in its context, our response of obedience must follow. The question each of us must ask is, "What is the truth that God wants me to act on?" To make this process concrete, journaling or writing can bring an added dimension.

WRITING INSIGHTS AND APPLICATIONS

As God opens your eyes to His insights, record them in written form. First, record a statement or statements of what the Holy Spirit has shown you. Second, record the passage that God used in teaching you this insight. An insight is not just a feeling or opinion, but a God-directed infiltration into your heart and mind to change the thoughts, actions, attitudes, etc., in your life. With it comes the ring of truth, knowing what is right, followed by the invitation to obedience.

Application naturally follows the insights that God has opened to you in His Word. However, they are not a result of your work any more than the insights. Rather, they are God's truth applied to your life, and your response of obedience to Him. The following is an example taken from the study of the book of Jonah.

> I see God asking Jonah to be obedient in spite of a lack of understanding on Jonah's part. Jonah was told to go to Nineveh and proclaim a message he had not yet received.
>
> > 1:1-2 The word of the Lord came to Jonah . . . "Arise, go to Nineveh the great city, and cry against it, for their wickedness has come up before Me."
> > 3:1-2 Now the Word of the Lord came to Jonah the second time, saying, "Arise, go to Nineveh the great city and proclaim to it the proclamation which I am going to tell you."
> > 3:4 Then Jonah began to go through the city one day's walk; and he cried out and said, "Yet forty days and Nineveh will be overthrown."
>
> God is showing me that I do not need to completely understand what I am to do and say before I begin to be obedient to the Word of God. God sent Jonah to Nineveh but did not give him the specific words to proclaim until He knew the time was right. My desire is to be obedient to the truth I understand and to trust the Lord for His timing for any further direction. Lord . . .

The above application illustrates one of the first insights I received in studying Jonah. The verses support the initial statement of insight, followed by the application of that insight to my thought processes and behavior. It may be that application insists upon some kind of specific action. Application can be a variety of things—mindset changed, thought patterns rearranged, behavior/conversations altered. In concluding the application, a prayer could be written to God acknowledging what He has said.

EXERCISE

Psalm 1 is divided into two paragraphs. Divide a piece of paper into two columns and answer the three basic questions: (1) Who are the characters and what are they doing? (2) What is the main idea? (3) Why is this important? What insights did you receive from Psalm 1 by studying it this way?

SYNTHESIS – THEME CHART

So far our study has involved observing the facts and their arrangement, and experiencing the Holy Spirit's explanation of the meaning and the inter-relatedness of these facts. The next step is to see these observations in relation to each other as a comprehensive whole. Unless we see the parts in their relationship to the whole, we will not fully understand the author's overall message.

Just as the unsightly seams on the inside of a garment secure the binding of the material together, synthesis is the bringing together of observed facts so that both content and arrangement of the Biblical portions are revealed. This will be recorded on a theme chart, thus portraying the flow and relationships of the themes with one another and with the entire book as well as becoming an invaluable memory aid.

As you study, the Lord has been applying His Word to you in specific ways. What are these persistent themes that God has been communicating to you? The chart will help you organize these themes and put the book back together. Keep in mind that your chart is to show observations that will lead to major insights.

INSTRUCTION FOR MAKING A THEME CHART:

1. To communicate the basic content of a portion of Scripture, the paragraph titles (main ideas) from your first observation chart will be written at the top of the theme chart in the designated area.

2. On the bases of these paragraph titles, develop chapter titles. Record chapter titles at the top of the chart under "Chapter Title."

3. At the very top of your chart write a title for the entire book. This title would best summarize the overall message of the book. The paragraph titles, chapter titles, and book title then become your outline (though not in typical outline format).

4. Select the verse that best illustrates the title and overall message of the book and write it at the bottom of your chart. This is your key verse.

5. Choose the themes that the Lord has been revealing to you throughout the Scripture. (These are themes that have surfaced repeatedly.) Often your observations on repetitions will expose themes. Simply ask the question, "What recurring themes has God communicated to me?"

6. Under "Themes" list the themes you intend to trace throughout the book. Then, summarize what the paragraph says about that theme by asking the question, "What does this paragraph have to say about the theme of _____?" Record your observations in the appropriate paragraph slot. Remember, not every paragraph will speak about each theme. Write a summary in your own words.

7. Further observations may be done by looking at some "general themes," which would include the Christian walk, the church, a doctrine such as salvation, etc. Thus, the question would be, "What does the paragraph have to say about the Christian walk/church?"

An example of a theme chart based on Philippians is found on pages 42-45.

EXERCISE

After observing the theme chart, make observations concerning the development of some of the themes and the relationship of one theme to another. Record your observations on the chart.

CORRELATION

As you study the Scriptures, God will deepen what He has already taught you by developing an unfolding picture of His Story. The continual process of revelation noting God's revelations of insights throughout the Bible is correlation—a lifelong process of God's building His truth into you. Even as you continue learning, you can speak authoritatively about what God has revealed to you from His Word. As Followers of Christ, our authority comes from Him as we share God's interpretations from the Word and not our own.

Correlation will naturally follow a study of Scripture, since the Lord will bring to your mind other portions of Scripture that expand and strengthen the interpretations and applications He has given you. Remember to do an historical background study of the Scripture, read the preceding and following chapters as well as any parallel texts to add to your contextual understanding of the correlated Scripture.

Be careful as you do correlative studies not to prove what you <u>think</u> you saw in the original portion studied. Each new portion of Scripture that is correlated to the original portion should be studied as well. Often the single verse reference, given in some Bibles in the small middle column or off to the side, attempts to connect an isolated verse with another verse without a strong relationship between the passages. For example, correlating Psalm 1:3 with John 15 might not be the best passage to increase understanding. One can never be conclusive about further interpretations unless the total context of the new portion has been inductively studied.

The following are examples from Philippians when correlated with Isaiah 53.

PHILIPPIANS	CORRELATION	ISAIAH 53
2:17 - "drink offering"	offering concept	v. 10 - guilt offering
1:5 - "partnership in the gospel"	response to message asking who believes our message	v. 1 - question being

EXERCISE

What passages could be correlated to Psalm 1?

Optional Exercise: Practice the guidelines found in this chapter by doing your own study using these principles on a short book of the Bible, such as Philemon.

THEME CHART

PHILIPPIANS

Book title: Philippians: Gospel Brings Joy

CHAPTER TITLES	Partners in the Gospel			
PARAGRAPH TITLES	1:1-2 Grace & Peace	1:3-11 Prayer & Thanks	1:12-18b Motives of Preaching	1:18c-26 To Live or To Die
THEME Joy, Rejoice		Pray with joy; prayer: love may abound	Rejoice in Christ being preached	Rejoice knowing that Christ will be exalted! Your progress & joy in the faith
THEME Gospel		Pray because partnership in Gospel; defending or sharing Gospel	Events in Paul's life advance Gospel; Paul here to defend Gospel	
THEME Ministry	"Together with overseers and deacons"	"Partnership"	Adverse events bring courage to speak God's word; motives of preaching	
THEME Life / Death				Christ exalted whether by life or death; struggle Life = Christ; death = gain
THEME Unity				

Key verse: 2:2 - "then make my joy complete by being ..."

		Christ's Attitude Found in Serving Others		
1:27-30 Standing Firm	2:!-11 Joy in Christ's Example	2:12-18 God's Work in You	2:19-24 Concern for Them	2:25-30 Info on Epaphroditus
	How to make complete joy	Paul's glad to be poured out. Church be glad & rejoice with Paul	Be cheered when I hear news about you	You be glad to see Epaphroditus Welcome him
Conduct to be worthy of Gospel; contending for faith of Gospel	Demonstrates Gospel in action of Christ			
Suffering & struggle is part of ministry	"Taking the nature of a servant"	God works in you. Hold out word of life.	Timothy—a fellow-servant in ministry	Epaphroditus— fellow worker, soldier & messenger
	Christ obedient to death—death on cross			Epaphroditus almost died
Standing firm in one spirit	United w/ Christ, one spirit			

THEME CHART

PHILIPPIANS (CONTINUED)
Book title: Philippians: Gospel Brings Joy

CHAPTER TITLES	Lost, to Press On		The Basics: Unity, Joy, Contentment	
PARAGRAPH TITLES	3:1-11 Fleshly Confidence Lost	3:12-21 Pressing on in Christ	4:1-3 Stand Firm in Unity	4:4-9 Rejoice, Think before Do
THEME Joy, Rejoice	Rejoice in the Lord		Church is Paul's joy	Rejoice in Lord always
THEME Gospel		Provides a pattern by which one can live	Worked with Paul for cause of the Gospel	What you have learned, practice
THEME Ministry	Self-righteousness of law contrasted with faith in Christ	Pressing on to win the prize God has called me — Paul modeling	Worked in ministry	
THEME Life / Death	Attain the resurrection of the dead	Enemies of cross destroyed	Names in Book of Life	
THEME Unity			Women agree with each other	

The Basics: Unity, Joy, Contentment			Observations/ Comments
4:10-13 Being Content	4:14-19 Fragrant Offerings	4:20-23 Final Greetings	Major or Minor Theme?
Paul rejoices greatly in Lord			Major theme – found in 69% of the paragraphs; theme connected with people; theme repeats itself
	In early days of Gospel, they shared with Paul		Strong theme in chapters 1 & 4 Gospel & ministry found in same paragraphs
Christ's strength required for ministry	Sharing of Trouble		Major theme in book as it is connected with gospel
			Minor theme; often connected to theme of joy, rejoice
Standing firm in one spirit			Minor theme; always connected with theme of gospel

CHAPTER FOUR

CONTEXTUAL BACKGROUNDS

INTRODUCTION TO BACKGROUND STUDIES

Two church members left after the sermon, when one asked the other, "Who was that Gomorrah that the pastor referred to?" The other responded, "I don't know but what is the relationship between Abram and Abraham? Were they twins?"

Understanding the context is basic to understanding our world. When events and experiences are disconnected from their context, meaning is often lost and the importance of the events or experiences is often diminished with anticipation for the next experience that moves to the forefront of the mind. Thus, the connecting tissue that gives meaning to life and its process is lost to the future.

Contextual backgrounds can be divided into numerous categories such as historical, literary, cultural, geographical, theological, sociological, etc. The purpose of this chapter is to establish a basic outline for background studies that integrate and incorporate these categories. Today we are blessed with numerous resources to understand the world of the Bible, but we must have discernment and wisdom in the use of these resources. With the proliferation of web sites and the decrease in documentation of original sources, our research must be vigilant. For your convenience, I have listed trustworthy Bible reference tools and have briefly explained their function and importance in the work of Bible study.

BACKGROUND WORKSHEETS

The basic background worksheet is found on page 25 in chapter three. We can expand this worksheet by asking additional questions. This chart asks two types of questions:

1. **Internal.** What does that specific book or the Bible have to say as to the historical context and times?
2. **External.** What do other sources (sources outside of the Bible) have to say about this book, people, towns, history, etc.?

Each of the basic five questions can be answered by looking at the text itself or elsewhere in the Bible. Each of these five basic questions can be further investigated with the following questions:

Author: Who wrote the book?
- What is known about this person from other writings?
- At what point in his life does this take place?
- What was the author's occupation?
- Where did he live?
- Who were his parents?
- What does his name mean? (Use a Bible dictionary.)

Recipients: To whom was the book written?
- Are the recipients specifically stated? If not, why not?
- What previous contact did they have with the author?
- Are the recipients seen elsewhere in Scripture?
- What kinds of people were they? What was their reputation?
- What other people are mentioned in the book? What is the relationship between the recipient and these people?

Location: From where was the book written?
- Where was the destination of the book?
- What is known about this location today?
- What other historical events happened here?
- What other locations are mentioned in this book?
- What can you find about each location?

Date: When was the book written?
- What other events were occurring at this time?
- Who were the world rulers at the time?
- Describe the rulers. What was their reputation?

Purpose: Why was the book written?
- What was the author's purpose?
- Is the purpose stated clearly? If not, what appears to be the purpose? Why is it not stated clearly? What would you say is the purpose?
- What do others say is the purpose? (Consult external sources.)
- What is the content of the book in relation to the stated purpose?
- What was the occasion that motivated the author?

How are these questions to be answered? First, allow the reading of the text to answer any of these questions. This is the evidence found in the Scriptures (the internal evidence). When the internal evidence does not answer the questions, then outside materials (external sources) are needed. For example, to answer the question who wrote Colossians is effortless, as it is stated in the first few verses. However, the same question applied to Jonah generates a search outside of the biblical text. When using external sources, make sure documentation is given, which is helpful if the sources need to be consulted later. Not only are there additional questions on "Background Worksheet B" (page 53), there is an additional question regarding literary genre (type). This question seeks to answer the general literal genre of the book. Knowing the genre assists in understanding what the author has written.

INTERNAL EVIDENCE	EXTERNAL EVIDENCE
Found as the book is read	Not found in the book or the Bible
Answers are evident in the text	Requires outside sources
Chapter and verse references given	Documentation of source given

TOOLS TO USE FOR FINDING
ANSWERS IN EXTERNAL EVIDENCE

Although books and resources seem to be in endless supply in our society today, every student of the Word needs certain books or tools that are close at hand, whether in paper or electronic form. In the remainder of this chapter, Bible reference tools will be briefly explained.

There are five necessary types of reference tools:

1. Bible dictionaries
2. Concordances
3. Books on customs and manners
4. Bible atlases
5. Bible handbooks

For each of these types there will be a description, ideas for use, and discussion of its importance within the scope of Bible study.

1. BIBLE DICTIONARIES

The Bible dictionary is a basic tool arranged alphabetically (as a regular dictionary), but with its focus on people, places, measurements, weights, theological doctrines, historical and literary introductions, words, customs, overviews of the books of the Bible, etc. Usually maps and illustrations are included to aid understanding. This tool often includes a helpful bibliography after each entry for further study and investigation. One major disadvantage is that the Bible student may miss some of the important material in a passage since it was not researched. Usually, there is no scriptural index to assist with research in a Bible dictionary. However, the Bible dictionary needs to be one of the first reference tools in a personal library as it encompasses, to one degree or another, all the elements of the other tools. The following list includes resources that I like to use.

- *The New Bible Dictionary* by J. Douglas, ed.
- *The Zondervan Pictorial Bible Dictionary* by Merrill Tenney, ed.
- *New Unger's Bible Dictionary* by R. K. Harrison, ed.
- *Smith's Bible Dictionary* by William Smith
- *Holman Bible Dictionary* by Trent C. Butler, ed.

Going a step further from the dictionary, including more information and greater detail, is the Bible encyclopedia. Although there are many good sets, two that I enjoy using are these:

- *The International Standard Bible Encyclopedia*
- *The Zondervan Pictorial Encyclopedia of the Bible* by Merrill C. Tenney, ed.

There are also some good dictionaries that deal with the study of Hebrew and Greek words. These sources assume the reader has some knowledge of the biblical languages as it gives the Hebrew or Greek word respectively.

- *Wilson's Old Testament Word Studies* by William Wilson
- *An Expository Dictionary of New Testament Words* by W.E. Vine

2. CONCORDANCES

The concordance is a massive volume that arranges words in alphabetical order. It lists all the English terms that have been used to translate a single word from the Greek or Hebrew. This tool shows where that word is found in the Bible and the Hebrew or Greek root word. It is a helpful tool for word studies. Although a theme can be traced throughout a book or the entire Bible, topical studies will naturally emerge from personal study as you synthesize the book or passage. One use for this tool is to check repetitions when you are studying a book or passage. The concordance will indicate whether or not all words were found.

Concordances vary according to the Biblical translation. There are concordances based on the KJV, NIV, NASV, and others. Get a concordance that matches the translation you use.

- *New American Standard Exhaustive Concordance of the Bible* by Robert L. Thomas, ed.
- *Young's Analytical Concordance to the Bible (KJV)* by Robert Young
- *Strong's Exhaustive Concordance of the Bible (KJV)* by James Strong
- *A Complete Concordance to the Holy Scripture of the Old Testament and New Testament* by Alexander Cruden

3. BOOKS ON CUSTOMS AND MANNERS

These books explain the customs and manners common in Bible days, which are foreign to us today. This tool helps us understand people who were different from us. Understanding historic customs is essential to an accurate understanding of the Scripture.

- *Manners and Customs in the Bible* by Victor Matthews, revised edition
- *The New Manners and Customs of Bible Times* by Fred Wight and Ralph Gower
- *Today's Handbook of Bible Times and Customs* by William Coleman
- *Sketches of Jewish Social Life in the Days of Christ* by Alfred Edersheim
- *Manners and Customs of the Bible* by James Freeman
- *Poet and Peasant and Through Peasant Eyes: A Literary-Cultural Approach to the Parables in Luke* by Kenneth E. Bailey

4. BIBLE ATLASES

A Bible atlas gives attention to the geography of the Bible world. Maps, drawings, topography, kingdom boundaries, journeys of various Bible characters, photographs of cities, temples, battles, etc., are all important in understanding the geography and history of the Bible. (In reading maps, do not forget to consult the key.) Many Bibles and Bible dictionaries have maps, but a good atlas is beneficial for giving more details than a Bible dictionary does.

- *The Macmillan Bible Atlas* by Yohanan Aharoni and Michael Avi-Yonah
- *The Zondervan Pictorial Bible Atlas* by E.M. Blaiklock, ed.
- *Hammond's Atlas of the Bible Lands*
- *The Moody Atlas of Bible Lands* by Barry J. Bietzel

5. BIBLE HANDBOOKS

A handbook is for the generalist because it provides background knowledge on each book of the Bible, as well as other important information. Often notes on difficult passages are provided to help create understanding. A handbook will touch on many things—overview of a book, historical information, important archaeological discoveries, etc.—and it will also function as a Bible dictionary. The format of the handbook usually follows the same book sequence as the Bible. Handbooks are unique in that they often offer an eclectic approach to information that can only be found by investigating all the other study tools. Unique items may be determined by consulting the table of contents or the index.

- *Eerdman's Handbook to the Bible* by David Alexander, ed.
- *Halley's Bible Handbook* by H. H. Halley
- *New Unger's Bible Handbook* revised by Gary N. Larson

A WORD ABOUT COMMENTARIES

Often students of the Bible seek information in a commentary first rather than last. Commentaries are the result of people studying the text and then making comments about the text—they analyze and then explain the text. Although there are many helpful commentaries, the sequence of consultation is usually the problem. Each student of the Bible must do his/her work first before seeking the assistance of a commentary. As the Bible student studies, questions are inevitable. Often the process of study will result in answers, but when that does not happen, then consult three or four good commentaries that might give insight into your questions. Sometimes commentaries confirm understanding, or they might give a completely different view, or they might not help at all! Beginning with your own study creates ownership of the text rather than initially listening to what someone else says.

SUMMARY

A background chart with questions is found on page 53. On page 54 is a "Bible Study Tool Search Chart" to give direction on which tools are possible resource materials for the question or item being sought.

EXERCISE

Choose two tools and investigate a passage of Scripture of your choice. Or, use Psalm 1 and see if any of these tools have helpful information to enrich your understanding of that passage. Perhaps, you could look up some of the words (e.g. "trees") in a Bible dictionary.

BACKGROUND WORKSHEET B

Book of the Bible: _____

INTERNAL EVIDENCE *What does book say?**	EXTERNAL EVIDENCE *What do external sources say?**
1. Author: Who wrote the book? • What is known about this person from other writings? • At what point in his life does this take place? • What was the author's occupation? What does his name mean? • Where did he live? Who was his father? • What changes have occurred since the author first appeared in the scriptures?	
2. Recipients: To whom was this book written? • Are the recipients specifically stated? If not, why not? • What previous contact did they have with the author? • Are the recipients seen elsewhere in Scripture? • What kinds of people were they? What was their reputation? • What other people are mentioned?	
3. Location: From where was the book written? • Where was the destination of the book? What is known about this location today? • What other historical events happened here? • What other locations are mentioned in this book? • What can you find about each location?	
4. Date: When was the book written? • What other events were occurring at this time? • Who were the world rulers at the time? • Describe the rulers. What was their reputation?	
5. Purpose: Why was the book written? • What was the purpose of the author? • Is the purpose stated clearly? If not, what appears to be the purpose? Why is it not stated clearly? What would you say is the purpose? • What do others say is the purpose? • What is the content of the book in relation to the stated purpose? • What was the occasion that motivated the writer?	

*Document your sources/references

BIBLE STUDY TOOL SEARCH CHART

Key: ☆ = Helpful; ☆☆ = More helpful

SEARCH FOR	CONCOR-DANCE	BIBLE DICTIONARY	CUSTOMS & MANNERS	ATLAS	BIBLE HANDBOOK
Archaeological discovery notes				☆	☆
Author information		☆☆			☆
Background information		☆	☆		☆
Buildings or Construction		☆	☆☆		
Church history summary					☆
City: historical account of a city		☆		☆	
Clothing and dress		☆	☆☆		
Cross references	☆				
Distance from one place to another				☆	
Food and diet		☆	☆☆		
Location of city, region, etc.		☆		☆☆	
Notes on difficult to understand passage					☆
Overview of book in Bible		☆			☆
Summary of topic		☆			
Temple diagram		☆☆			☆
Theme development	☆				
Topic of "trust"	☆				
Topography of land, e.g. altitude changes				☆	
Verse when only one word is known	☆				
Word etymology	☆☆	☆			
Words unique to passage, e.g. Urim and Thummin		☆			

CHAPTER FIVE

OBSERVATIONS: SEEING WHAT'S THERE!

INTRODUCTION

"When did they build that house?" was my question one day as I traveled my usual route. I was driving that same highway three times a week, but I did not remember seeing that yellow house. Had it just been built? Had I not seen it before? Or, was I simply looking without seeing? How often do I fail to observe what is there? Yet, observations are endless. When do our eyes take it all in? Looking, looking again, and looking again bring additional insights to the Scriptures. This chapter builds on what has already been stated. Substantial observations require time and perseverance in the discipline of searching the Scriptures; such observing produces easier interpretation. But first, we need to recognize some tendencies.

1. Do not get lost in the details. Not everything is important. Select items that are important. (This is learned through Bible study experience!)
2. Do not stop with observations, but also ask questions and seek answers.
3. Do not give everything equal weight; discern what is important. (Again, time and experience will help.)

Now that you are acquainted with the basics (as found in chapter 3), what more can be built upon this foundation? The purpose of this chapter is to provide observation alternatives in developing a mind that observes, asks questions, and stimulates further insights as eyes are opened to the Word.

BUILDING ON OBSERVATIONS
(from the three-column worksheet)

The following worksheets and charts provide additional ideas and options in working with the observation worksheet #1, first introduced in chapter 3.

OBSERVATION 1
Variations from the Basic Three-Column Observation Worksheet

WHO? WHAT? Who are the characters? What are they doing/saying?	MAIN IDEA What is the main idea of the paragraph?	WHY? What is the significance of the main idea?
• Note the adjectives used to describe the nouns. Underline them with a specific color • Note the verbs. Are they passive? Active? Use specific colors to note this. • Look through preceding paragraphs and locate new characters. Underline or circle major characters.	• Rather than 5 words, limit the title to 4, or 3, or 2, or 1 word. • Include the key word or repeated words in the title. • Begin each paragraph with the same letter of the alphabet.	• How would this text read if this paragraph was not here? • At times a cause and effect (C & E) statement will state a purpose or the significance of the paragraph. Do you see any C & E statements that help with the significance?

EXPLANATION OF ADDITIONAL OBSERVATION WORKSHEETS

The following pages are variations on the basic observation worksheet. The chart below explains adaptations of this basic worksheet. Various features of these worksheets are listed below. Again, develop your own observation worksheet.

NAME OF OBSERVATION WORKSHEET	SPECIAL FEATURE	GOOD FOR WHAT BOOKS OF THE BIBLE
Observation #1-A: **The Five W's** (page 58)	• What? What is the action of the paragraph? • Who? Who are the characters in the paragraph? • When? When is this happening? • Where? Where is this action taking place? • Why? Why is this paragraph important?	This worksheet can be used with most books of the Bible; however, since places and locations are found in historical and/or narrative books, this worksheet answers the important "where" question.
Observation #1-B: **Focus on Action** (page 59)	Focus on the *action* of the paragraph	Acts, Gospels, historical books of the OT
Observation #1-C: **Unstructured Approach** Based on Oletta Wald's book, *The Joy of Discovery* (page 60)	More unstructured approach, focusing on passages making general or specific observations, and asking questions for understanding	All scripture
Observation #1-D: **Traina's Observation Analysis** (page 61)	A more technical worksheet that focuses on terms found in the scriptures and the structure of terms with the text of the passage. It also addresses the atmosphere (mood) of the passage.	All scripture

WORKSHEETS ONLINE

All of the worksheets in the book are available as full-sheet versions at the book web site. You can use these versions in the classroom or for your own study.

www.dennisfledderjohann.com

WORKSHEET

OBSERVATION #1-A: THE 5 W'S

Reference _____ Chapter/Section Title _____

WHO?	WHAT?	WHERE?	WHEN?	WHY?

WORKSHEET

OBSERVATION #1-B: FOCUS ON ACTION

Reference _____ Chapter/Section Title _____

WHO?	WHAT: ACTION?	WHERE?	WHEN?	WHY: SIGNIFICANCE

WORKSHEET

OBSERVATION #1-C: UNSTRUCTURED WORKSHEET[7]

SCRIPTURE PASSAGE	OBSERVATIONS	QUESTIONS FOR UNDERSTANDING

7. Based on *The Joy of Discovery in Bible Study* by Oletta Wald

WORKSHEET

OBSERVATION #1-D:
TRAINA'S OBSERVATION ANALYSIS[8]

SCRIPTURE	TERMS	STRUCTURE BETWEEN TERMS	ATMOSPHERE
Scripture studied is recorded here.	Observation of any given word in this passage. • Is this term routine? • Is it unusual? • Is it figurative? • What grammatical category is it—noun, verb, adjective, adverb, preposition, etc.? • Is it singular or plural?	Observe the relationships between the terms. • Structural units— phrases, clauses, sentences, paragraphs, etc. • Paragraph relationships—relation of subject to verb, verb to complete predicate, etc. • Sentence relationships—direct object, modifiers, conjunctions, connectives, etc. • How are things arranged? • What are the verb tenses?	What is the underlying mood or spirit of this passage? • Despair? • Thanksgiving? • Awe? • Urgency? • Joy? • Humility? • Tenderness? • Etc.

8. Source: *Methodical Bible Study* by Robert Traina, pp. 33+

BUILDING ON THE FORMS OF EXPRESSION

Six basic forms of expression have already been listed. Several of these can be expanded as demonstrated below.

1. Building on Repetitions

Because of the importance and nature of repetitions in Scripture, underlining in green the words, phrases, concepts, and themes may become very confusing. Therefore, the following is another design to be considered. Rather than green underlining, simply develop a green code of different shaped markings. The following illustrates this idea.

WORD	DESCRIPTION	REPETITION MARKED BY
God	triangle or theta (Greek letter for God)	Θ
righteousness	abbreviate with "RT"	RT or rt
love	draw a heart with an arrow through it	♥
grace	mark with a capital "G"	G

2. Building on Additional Color Coding

Additional colors (as indicated below) may be added to the existing six colors to afford more observations.

COLOR	OBSERVATIONS NOTED
Yellow	Commands/imperatives
Purple	Promises

Rather than using colors to identify forms of expressions, you may also use colors for topics, such as indicated below.

COLOR	SCRIPTURE PASSAGES THAT ADDRESS
Green	the Christian walk
Red	the blood, cross, the work of Jesus Christ
Yellow	the work of the Holy Spirit
Black	sin, evil, Satan, etc.
Light Blue	eternal life, God's eternal kingdom

Another idea is to identify the major topics in the book with various colors.

BUILDING ON THE LARGER FORMS OF EXPRESSIONS

Not only are there specific, individual forms of expression scattered throughout the chapters, there are also larger ones. Main forms of expressions are found in chapters and books. One must step back to see the larger picture of each form. Some are quickly seen; others are not evident at all! Allow the text to speak for itself! These charts are helpful when looking at the major forms of expression in respect to the chapter and to the book in its entirety. Observation worksheets #2-A and #2-B are found on the following pages.

WORKSHEETS ONLINE

All of the worksheets in the book are available as full-sheet versions at the book web site. You can use these versions in the classroom or for your own study.

www.dennisfledderjohann.com

OBSERVATION CHART #2-A:
SUMMARY OF FORMS OF EXPRESSION

Guiding questions: What is the major form of expressions in this chapter?

CHAPTER	COMPARI-SON	CON-TRASTS	REPETI-TIONS	CAUSE & EFFECT	PROGRES-SIONS & LISTS	SUMMARY STATE-MENTS
Chap. 1						
Chap. 2						
Chap. 3						
Chap. 4						
Conclu-sions (Which of these are the major ones?)						

OBSERVATION CHART #2-B:
BOOK SUMMARY OF FORMS OF EXPRESSION

Book _____

Guiding question: What is the major <u>form of expression</u> in this book?

Comparison:

Contrast:

Repetition:

Cause and Effect:

Progression:

Summary Statement:

Observations/Conclusions: What form of expression is the dominant one found in this book?

GOING BEYOND THE FORMS OF EXPRESSION TO LITERARY FORMS

Forms of expression are the general forms of language that everyone uses. Literary forms are more specific and are related to the study of analyzing literature, particularly poetry. The following list introduces six common literary forms.

LITERARY FORM	EXPLANATION/DESCRIPTION	EXAMPLE
Apostrophe	It is addressing things/people as being present though they are absent. Jesus addressed the citizens of towns though they were not present.	Matthew 11:21—"Woe to you, Korazin! Woe to you, Bethsaida! If the miracles that were performed in you had been performed in Tyre and Sidon, they would have repented long ago in sackcloth and ashes."
Euphemism	Euphemism is using pleasant words or phrases for that which is unpleasant, repulsive or inappropriate.	For example, "He is gone to be with the Lord," "She passed away," or "She went home," meaning heaven.
Hyperbole	Hyperbole is an exaggeration that is made in order to convey a thought.	Matthew 23:24—"You blind guides! You strain at a gnat but swallow a camel."
Metonymy	Metonymy is the use of one word for another word that it suggests. The word names a thing by one of its attributes or accompaniments.	Luke 4:43—"But he said, 'I must preach the good news of the kingdom of God to the other towns also, because that is why I was sent.'" Matthew 16:19—"I will give you the keys of the kingdom of heaven; whatever you bind on earth will be bound in heaven, and whatever you loose on earth will be loosed in heaven."
Personification	Personification is giving an object a personality or the characteristics of a human being.	John 3:8—"The wind blows wherever it pleases. You hear its sound, but you cannot tell where it comes from or where it is going. So it is with everyone born of the Spirit."
Similes[9] and Metaphors	Similes use the words "like" or "as" to indicate a comparison. Metaphors do not use the words "like" or "as" to indicate a comparison.	Simile in Psalm 1: "And he shall be like a tree planted by streams of water . . . ." Metaphor in Luke 13:32—He replied, "Go tell that fox, 'I will drive out demons'. . . ." John 15:1—"I am the true vine, and my Father is the gardener."

Additional literary forms can be found in *Living by the Book*, pp. 271-272.

9. In our "Forms of Expression" what was called a "comparison" was in reality a "simile."

QUESTION BUILDERS:
PRINCIPLES ON WHICH TO BUILD QUESTIONS

One essential for discovery is the ability to ask questions. In order to cultivate the ability to ask good questions, we first need to ask why questions are important. Questions are important because they (1) aid the process of understanding in the learning experience, (2) provoke us to think and build upon our thinking, and (3) encourage further research and discussion. The following principles can be used to ask questions in various areas.

1. Quantity Principle

How many verses has the author used to describe a topic, idea, concept, event, situation, etc.? Often the quantity of material indicates the value of material. Ask, "What does this say? What does this imply?"

2. Time Principle

How much time has transpired in this verse? paragraph? chapter? book? When can this be dated (month and year)? What other important events were occurring/people were living at this time? How does this "time" help us with the other parts of the book?

3. Relationship Principle

What are the relationships between verses, chapters, paragraphs, words, verb tenses, before and after events, etc.? How are things arranged? Look at the connectives (conjunctions), prepositions, clauses, pronouns, etc. Look for changes. Compare the beginning with the end of the book. How does the passage naturally divide?

4. Omission Principle

Why did the author select the material used? Why was this included and not something else? If this had been omitted, would it imply a lack of importance? Why?

5. People Principle

What do their names mean? Have those names occurred before? If so, where? What do other Scriptures say about these people? What reputation do they have?

6. Events or Historical Principle

Has a similar event occurred at another time? What makes this event distinct from other events? What cause and effect does this event have on the flow of history?

7. Geographical Principle

What does this name mean? How did it receive this meaning? What important events took place here? Where is it today? What is it like today? Has archeological study been done on this place? If so, what?

ANSWERING QUESTIONS

How does one find answers to questions like these? First, be diligent in your study by making accurate observations. For example, know the difference between conjunctions and prepositions. Second, strong observations can help to make better implications. For example, in responding to questions under the omission principle, subjectivity enters into the reason why the author selected the material used, but good observations lead to strong implications. Third, use external resources such as a Bible dictionary or a Bible encyclopedia for meanings of names or places. *Use commentaries only after personally studying the passage.*

OBSERVATIONS ON GRAMMAR ANALYSIS

Words placed in a certain order create sentences. The study of phrase and sentence structure is called syntax. Proper grammar follows the syntactic rules of a language. When this does not occur, sentences do not make sense. Our observations can gain greater meaning when grammar and syntax are inspected. The following ideas will aid the focus on this area.

The basic observation chart includes characters (Who?) and action (What?) in the first column. As you consider these, other things can be observed. Possibly during elementary school you studied sentence diagramming. Though the teacher probably never said so, diagramming skills are applicable to Bible study. Much detail for an exercise could be given; I have given some of the basics for making observations on various parts of speech.

VERBS

1. **Tense.** What is the verb tense?
   - Present—It is occurring now. (Jesus *is* my Savior.)
   - Past—It happened before this moment. (Jesus *went* to the temple.)
   - Future—It will happen after this moment. (Jesus *will return.*)

2. **Voice.** Who is doing the action?
   - Active voice—Subject is doing the action. (*Paul* wrote letters.)

- Passive voice—Subject is receiving the action. (The letters were written by *Paul*.)

3. **Mood.** What is the mood of the verb?
   - Indicative—This mood expresses facts, opinions, or asks questions. It is the most common mood. (Jesus came to His disciples.)
   - Imperative—This mood gives orders or commands. (Come to me.)

NOUNS/PRONOUNS

1. **Person.** Is it first, second or third person pronouns?
   - First person—I, we, me, us
   - Second person—you
   - Third person—he, she, it, they, them

2. **Number.** Is it singular or plural?
   - Singular—One (A *woman* was healed.)
   - Plural—Two or more (Jesus healed many *people*.)

3. **Case.** In what case is the noun or pronoun used?
   - Subjective Case—the subject of sentences (*Jesus* lifted His hands.) (*He* looked toward his disciples.)
   - Objective Case—the receiver of action (Jesus lifted His *hands*.) (He looked toward *them*.)
   - Possessive Case—ownership (Jesus lifted *His* hands.) (The disciple took the *boy's* loaves and fish.)

Pay close attention to subjects and verbs; thus, observations concerning main idea and significance can easily be made, particularly when these are repeated within the paragraph. The following page is an example of what this looks like using Galatians 2:20-21.

WORKSHEET

GRAMMATICAL WORKSHEET:
GALATIANS 2:20-21 (NIV)

NOUNS AND PRONOUNS	VERBS	ADJ. AND ARTICLES	ADVERBS	CONJUNC-TIONS	PREP. PHRASES
Gal. 2:20					
[20] I have been crucified with Christ and I no longer live, but Christ lives in me. The life I live in the body, I live by faith in the Son of God, who loved me and gave himself for me.					
I — 4 times Christ me – 3 times life body faith Son God who Himself	have been crucified	the — 3 times	no longer	and — 2 times but	with Christ in me in the body by faith in the Son of God for me
	live — 4 times loved gave				
—focus is on the "I"	—focus on live, one passive verb				
Gal. 2:21					
[21] I do not set aside the grace of God, for if righteousness could be gained through the law, Christ died for nothing!"					
I grace God righteousness law Christ nothing	do set aside could be gained died	the — 2 times	not	for if	of God through the law for nothing

Notes and observations:
- This is a verb and noun passage.
- Christ works in people by virtue of the cross.
- Key words found in this passage—crucified, live, faith, righteousness, nothing, etc.
- Verse 20 focuses on life; verse 21 focuses on death.

WORSHEET

OBSERVATION EXERCISE

Exercise: Stretch Your Observations - look, Look, and LOOK AGAIN
Select either Psalm 23 or Matthew 28:18-20 and record as many observations as you can in three minutes! After twenty-four hours, repeat this exercise.

Book:_____ Passage:_____

1.

2.

3.

4.

5.

6.

7.

8.

9.

10.

11.

12.

13.

(After 24 hours, do it again! How many different ones can you discover?)

CHAPTER SIX

INTERPRETATION BUILDING PROCESS

INTERPRETATION BASICS

The Bible study process is designed so that the meaning of the text slowly emerges, coming to the surface of the learner's mind as the Holy Spirit teaches and illuminates. In order for this to occur, there first must be a trust in the Holy Spirit who opens minds, allowing the meaning of His Word to be taught. This requires coming to the text without preconceived ideas. Second, if the student has observed carefully, then proper interpretation happens. For example, knowing the purpose of the book helps to understand the text. Knowing the main ideas, repeated concepts, and major themes assists in comprehending the entire narrative, the movement and flow of the passage. Interpretation always follows observation, not vice versa! "Meaning Map #1" on the following page illustrates this concept.

The basic interpretation question is, "What does this mean to the original audience?" However, interpretation is not the only step toward answering this question; there are a number of questions in the discovery process.

1. What did the author mean when he wrote it?
2. What is the cultural background of this passage? (Use your Bible dictionary or customs book.)

MEANING MAP #1

The interactive study as previously explained has "built-in" guidelines for interpretation and understanding of the text.

HISTORICAL BACKGROUND ...
study gives author, recipients, location, date, and purpose, thus providing background understanding.

THE HEART OF BIBLE STUDY ...
is **interpretation** based on valid **observations** that give **application**. Observations formulate understanding to make application by the student of the Word.

SYNTHESIS ...
gives understanding of the flow and structure of the book, identifying major and minor themes and various relationships.

CORRELATION ...
gives understanding to the current text by the illumination of other texts more obvious and clear in meaning than possibly the text being studied.

THE FOUNDATION
Prayer. Seek the direction of the Holy Spirit.
Psalm 119:18 — "Open my eyes that I may see wonderful things in your law."

3. How was the original audience to respond?
4. Investigate critical terms (possibly word studies) on which the passage pivots.
5. What are the themes in this passage?
6. How do the themes relate to the issue at hand?
7. How does the author wish us to view this issue?
8. What present examples correspond to this passage?
9. What does it mean to us today? What relates directly to modern readers? What conveys an underlying principle to its modern readers? What does the passage mean now?

The following elements assist in this process of interpretation. Know the context of the passage:

1. **Historical Background**. The background study, one of the first areas of investigation, began this process.

2. **Cultural Background**. This background addresses the customs, mores, dress, and food preparation of that day. What is the cultural background of this passage? Use a Bible dictionary or customs book. As study continues, details will require the student to use basic Bible study tools to understand customs and words. Interpretation must always be within the historical and cultural background of the book being studied.

3. **Grammatical Context found in Paragraphs and Chapters**. Investigate critical terms (possibly word studies) on which the passage pivots. Unique words and sentence structures may assist understanding of the text. Sentence diagramming may be of assistance in such a case. When analyzing the text, use study tools such as lexicons, concordances, grammar books, word-study books, Bible dictionaries and encyclopedias, as well as commentaries.

COMMON-SENSE APPROACH TO UNDERSTANDING THE SCRIPTURE

1. Literally understand the text within context, unless this goes beyond general acceptable knowledge.
2. Write or record questions about the sections/pieces that do not make sense.
3. Words that are difficult to understand may be found in an English dictionary.

4. To assess understanding, paraphrase the passage in your own words and then compare it with a Bible paraphrase such as *The Message* or *The Living Bible*.

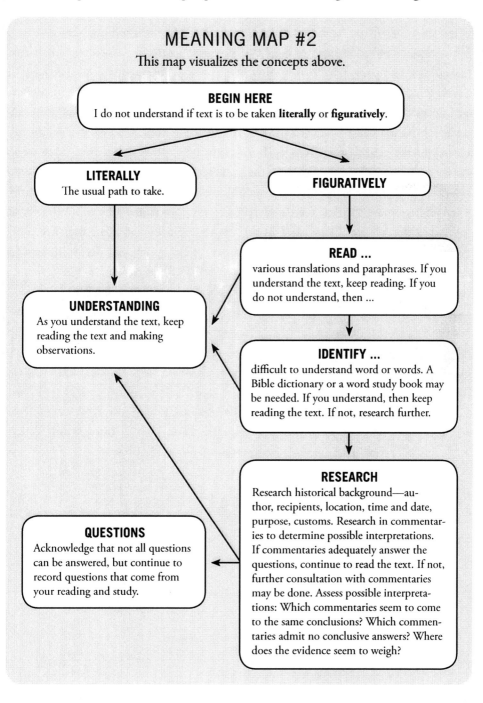

MEANING MAP #2
This map visualizes the concepts above.

BEGIN HERE
I do not understand if text is to be taken **literally** or **figuratively**.

LITERALLY
The usual path to take.

FIGURATIVELY

READ ...
various translations and paraphrases. If you understand the text, keep reading. If you do not understand, then ...

UNDERSTANDING
As you understand the text, keep reading the text and making observations.

IDENTIFY ...
difficult to understand word or words. A Bible dictionary or a word study book may be needed. If you understand, then keep reading the text. If not, research further.

RESEARCH
Research historical background—author, recipients, location, time and date, purpose, customs. Research in commentaries to determine possible interpretations. If commentaries adequately answer the questions, continue to read the text. If not, further consultation with commentaries may be done. Assess possible interpretations: Which commentaries seem to come to the same conclusions? Which commentaries admit no conclusive answers? Where does the evidence seem to weigh?

QUESTIONS
Acknowledge that not all questions can be answered, but continue to record questions that come from your reading and study.

GOING DEEPER: DISTINGUISHING BETWEEN FIGURATIVE AND LITERAL MEANINGS

The bottom line of understanding the Bible often rests on the question, "Is this to be understood literally or figuratively?" Sometimes the Bible will indicate that a passage is figurative by its redundancy of figurative language, its stated purpose or a correlated passage that gives direction in answering this question. Yet one question that *must* be answered is, "How did the original audience understand the passage?" Two guidelines are important to differentiate between the literal and the figurative: (1) the close examination of the text and its context, and (2) the use of the word or words in the immediate scriptural text and other passages. If the term is figurative, decide how it resembles the literal by identifying the figure. If the statement is out of character with the thing described, it is usually figurative. For example, a statement may be considered figurative when an inanimate object is used to describe a person or animate being. (When Jesus referred to Himself as a "Door" and "Bread," He was using figurative language.) At times the same word is used figuratively in one place and literally in another. This is the case for the word "lion" in 1 Peter 5:8 and Revelation 5:5. "Lion" means Satan in one place and refers to Jesus Christ in the second place. A word does not have a literal and figurative meaning at the same time. Begin with the literal meaning and if that interpretation does not agree, then the context will indicate its figurative meaning. "Meaning Map #3" on page 77 visualizes this concept. For example, Galatians 4 states that Mt. Sinai is a symbol of bondage and Jerusalem is a symbol of grace. These are literal geographical locations that are also symbols of spiritual truths.

The "Basic Genre Identification Worksheet" on page 78 gives further instructions when interpreting the type of genre in Scripture. Pages 79-81, "Interpreting Genres in the Bible," give hints on interpreting various genre of the Bible.

MEANING MAP #3

Basic Question: What does this mean?

Key Question: What did this passage mean to the original audience/recipients? (In order to answer this, knowledge of original recipients and historical setting of literature is needed.)

Assumption: God does not play hide 'n seek with us.

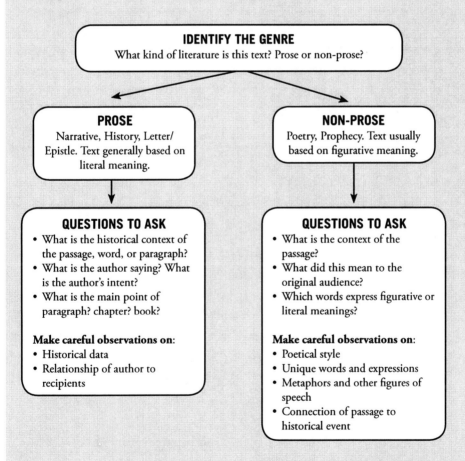

IDENTIFY THE GENRE
What kind of literature is this text? Prose or non-prose?

PROSE
Narrative, History, Letter/ Epistle. Text generally based on literal meaning.

NON-PROSE
Poetry, Prophecy. Text usually based on figurative meaning.

QUESTIONS TO ASK
- What is the historical context of the passage, word, or paragraph?
- What is the author saying? What is the author's intent?
- What is the main point of paragraph? chapter? book?

Make careful observations on:
- Historical data
- Relationship of author to recipients

QUESTIONS TO ASK
- What is the context of the passage?
- What did this mean to the original audience?
- Which words express figurative or literal meanings?

Make careful observations on:
- Poetical style
- Unique words and expressions
- Metaphors and other figures of speech
- Connection of passage to historical event

PRINCIPLES/TRUTHS
Application—generally to Body of Christ and specifically to individuals

WORKSHEET

BASIC GENRE IDENTIFICATION

Passage: _____

Answer the questions below by checking the "yes" or "no" column.

QUESTIONS	YES	NO
Does the passage appeal to the intellect?		
Does the thought progress in a sequential manner and come to some logical conclusion?		
Are exhortations and commands found in the passage?		
Are conclusions or some call-to-action found?		
Is descriptive, symbolic, and figurative language found?		
Is future prophecy presented?		
Are visions/dreams found in the passage?		
Are historical facts in the passage?		
Is there an appeal to the imagination with an emotional flavor?		
Are characters/people presented that develop the story line?		
Are characters/people presented in either a positive or a negative manner?		
Is figurative language meant to be taken literally?		
Are ideas repeated for the purpose of emphasis or contrast?		
Is the passage basically doctrine and theology?		

- If "yes" is checked for questions 1-4, 8, 13, and 14, then the literature is probably prose, discourse, epistle, and/or doctrine.
- If "yes" is checked for questions 1, 5-7, 9, and 13, then the literature is probably apocalyptic.
- If "yes" is checked for questions 9-11, then the literature is probably prose, narrative, story, and/or biographical.
- If "yes" is checked for questions 5, 9, 12-13, then the literature is probably poetry.

Genre identified as _____

What key paragraphs support your conclusion?

INTERPRETING GENRES IN THE BIBLE

Primary Sources: *How to Read the Bible for All Its Worth* by Gordon D. Fee and Douglas Stuart and *Living by the Book* by Hendricks.

TYPE	DEFINITION AND DESCRIPTION	HOW TO INTERPRET	EX.
Exposition	• Straightforward argument or explanation of passage that appeals to the mind. • Usually has a structure moving from point to point that often includes paragraphs linked with connectives (for, therefore, and, but, etc.) and rhetorical questions. The structure of a letter often includes name of writer, name of recipient, greeting, prayer and thanksgiving, body of letter, and the farewell or final greeting.	• Meaning lies close to the surface; appeals to logic, structure and order; truth is obvious; observe structure and terms that are used. • Use basic questions already stated in historical background and observation exercises.	Paul's letters, e.g. Romans
Narrative[10] Story, History, Biography	• Literature with people and places relating to historical direction. There is movement of action whether physical, spiritual, relational or political. • Stories have a setting, some sort of conflict (a place where the heart responds), a climax and resolution. • Remember that narratives do not answer all our questions about any given situation.	• Questions: What is the occasion? What is the flow of events? How is the story connected to the larger story of the book? of the Bible as a whole? What is happening? What is this illustrating? What kind of people are present? What did God do to and through these people? How does it end? What is allegorical? What theological issues are included? How can the reader vicariously live in the life of one of the characters? What can be learned from the character? Is there a moral? If so, what is it? • Pay attention to (1) Plot— what movement occurs in the story? What development occurs? What is different at the end of the book and why? (2) Characters—who are the characters? How are they represented? (3) In what way is the story true to life?[11]	Genesis Exodus (parts) Ruth Jonah Gospels Acts

TYPE	DEFINITION AND DESCRIPTION	HOW TO INTERPRET	EX.
Parables (metaphors and allegories)	• A parable is a tale (although parables can be facts or history) that illustrates a moral principle that is usually simple, memorable, and entertaining. Parables often include basic ethical principles of right and wrong, love and compassion, justice and mercy. • Metaphors are usually confined to a single word or sentence. • Allegories tend to be extended metaphors. Allegories mean something other than what is stated; another sense is expressed than that which the words convey; certain facts may be made to typify other truths; to set forth one thing in the image of another.	• Parables often use words in their literal sense. Parables are usually easy to understand as they deal with everyday, familiar matters. Also, Jesus explained parables to those who sought understanding. • Metaphors usually have one meaning. • Allegories are often figuratively used with application to some possible fact or historical event. • Questions: What did the parable mean to the original audience? What kind of parable is this—metaphor, epigram, allegory, etc.? What is the response to the parable by the original audience? How would this audience identify with the parable? What cultural customs within the parable need to be understood?	Parables in Matt. 13
Poetry	• Hebrew parallelism that includes repetition, additional new information, contrasts, and hyperbole. • Poetry appeals to the emotions and imagination and is often to be sung, not read.	• Questions: Who was the author? What was the occasion? What is the central theme of the poem? What kind of Hebrew poetry (parallelism) is present—synonymous (second line repeats first line), antithetical (second line contrasts first line), or synthetic (second line builds or adds to the first line)? What symbolism, metaphors, or hyperbole (exaggerations) are found in the poetry? What words or phrases are directed to the emotions? In which category would the poetry fit—lament, thanksgiving, worship, praise, wisdom, history, trust, etc.?	Psalms

10. In Gordon D. Fee and Douglas Stuart's book, *How to Read the Bible for all its Worth*, 3rd edition, "Principles for Interpreting Narratives" are given on page 106.
11. Additional questions may be found in *Living By the Book*, pages 216 and 217.

TYPE	DEFINITION AND DESCRIPTION	HOW TO INTERPRET	EX.
Proverbs or Wisdom Literature	• The writer assumes the role of an old wise man ready to share his insights to a younger, inexperienced, teachable person. • Proverbs are short, poignant nuggets of truth, typically practical and often concerned with the consequences of human behavior.	• Usually obvious and straight to the point. • Easy to understand but difficult to apply! • Questions would be similar to poetry questions but would include 1) What is the argument? 2) How is the argument laid out? 3) What figurative language is used? 4) How is this language to be understood in light of the context?	Proverbs
Prophecy and Apocalyptic Literature	• Contains the concept of foretelling the future and usually including warnings, predictions, and judgments. Be aware of multiple imagery in symbols (1 Pet. 5:8; Rev. 5:5; Matt. 5:13; Luke 14:34-35; Mark 9:49-50).	• Be cautious with this genre as it is the most challenging! Observe the natural qualities of the objects discussed and select the one parallel natural quality that the text intends. • Questions to ask: What is the historical context of the passage? What tense are verbs—past, present or future? What is the prophetic message? Were there blessings (life health, prosperity, agricultural abundance, respect, safety, etc.) or curses (death, disease, drought, danger, defeat, disgrace, etc.)? What symbols— visions, dreams or images—are in this passage? How are they to be understood? What countries are connected with this prophecy? What is the big picture? What problem is the passage addressing? What was the author's original meaning? What does the passage say about God? Use Bible study tools (Bible dictionaries, handbooks, and commentaries) to interpret prophetic passages.	Revelation Daniel (parts)

IDENTIFY THE PERMANENT PRINCIPLES

The events of Scripture happened in the past, yet God has given us principles that are forever permanent—ready to be applied in the present. A permanent principle is a truth or behavior, stated or implied, in the Word. It is a principle that all believers are responsible to do or be. It is a timeless truth embedded in the Word and found by proper study of the text. A question to ask is, "What is the principle of this passage?" Avoid finding a principle from every verse or paragraph. Principles will flow from the passage as a whole, centering on the main ideas and the repeated concepts. Of course, in some passages (particularly epistles) the principles are clear. In other passages (historical and stories), the principles are implied because of the action and behavior of characters. An implied principle must be consistent with the truth of the Bible as a whole. Permanent principles never change, while responses (applications) to the principle do change. When I obey the principles that I find in the Scriptures, the life of Christ comes alive within me; that is what God desires for us.

Words are always to be understood in their context. Words are seen in the context of the passage, the sentence, the paragraph, and the chapter. Scripture is to be interpreted in its natural, literal sense according to the ordinary rules of grammar. God is not in the business of hiding Himself from us. He is a God of revelation.

BEWARE OF DANGERS

Here are some common pitfalls that can occur at the interpretation stage.

1. An inadequate interpretation based on failing to validate the complete meaning of the text by seeing less than what is really there. Example: A person takes a trivial approach to celebrating the Lord's Supper, and serious self-examination is neglected (1 Corinthians 11:28-29).

2. An inflated interpretation based on assigning more meaning to the text than it warrants by seeing more than what is really there. Example: A person does not partake of the Lord's Supper for fear of bringing judgment upon him/herself (1 Corinthians 11:29-30).

3. An inaccurate interpretation when the wrong meaning is reached because of the lack of diligent study, or the failure to observe properly or to rely on the teaching ministry of the Holy Spirit. Example: Many current Christians understand the concept of church as a building rather than people. When used in conversation,

such as "We are going to church tomorrow. What are you doing?" their understanding of church is a location, a place to go to rather than being a part of the group of people known as the church.

4. An inaccurate interpretation of Scripture because one's personal experience is used to verify the meaning. In doing this, the standard of authority becomes experience. Example: Someone who had difficulty with overspending destroys all his credit cards. He is so successful in overcoming his problem that he insists that anyone not following Romans 13:8 by also destroying credit cards violates Scripture and thus is sinning. When this occurs, his experience rather than the Word has become the authority.

5. An inaccurate interpretation of Scripture results when popular philosophies and contemporary ideas are used to interpret passages. The Bible is not a science book, yet it deals with aspects related to scientific fields. Because the Bible is true, all that it contains is trustworthy. Example: With our technological age, some church groups telecast their services to satellite locations, and the prominent senior pastor presents the sermon. This contemporary influence denies the importance of the Body of Christ who received gifts and callings to function in ministry as seen in 1 Corinthians 12-14 and Ephesians 4.

6. A romanticized interpretation of the Scriptures results when one spiritualizes a passage, reading something into the text that is not evident. An example of this can be found in Acts 28 when Paul was bitten by a snake. To spiritualize this historical event is to say that the devil is always attacking righteous men, but he is always defeated. While the conclusion may be true, Acts 28 does not teach this conclusion.

SUMMARY

God is Revelation. His nature is to reveal Himself, so we may approach the Word with the expectation and excitement of knowing that God is going to reveal Himself in a unique and special way! May our response be in obedience and may it be done quickly! Page 85 is a worksheet that can be used for developing the interpretative process.

> Reflect on what I am saying, for the Lord will give you insight into all this.
>
> 2 Timothy 2:7

EXERCISE

Answer the following questions with the information that has already been stated.

1. Should Genesis 31:49 be used as a benediction? Why or why not?
2. What kind of healing does 1 Peter 2:24 speak of? Give rationale for your answer.
3. Is 1 Corinthians 2:9-10 speaking of heaven? Give rationale for your answer.
4. Romans 8:28 is often quoted. Is this what the Scripture is indeed saying? How do you explain this in the light of its context?
5. In Philippians 3:2, how does Paul use the term "dogs"?

EXERCISE

Select a passage of Scripture, which you have already studied, and answer the following questions:

1. What is the purpose and who was the original audience?
2. How was the original audience to respond?
3. What meaning did this Scripture have for the original audience?

WORKSHEET

TRAINA'S OBSERVATION-INTERPRETATION[12]

OBSERVATION: WHAT DO I SEE THAT IS DIFFICULT TO UNDERSTAND?	WHAT DOES THIS MEAN?	WHY IS THIS SAID? WHY IS IT SAID HERE?	IMPLICATIONS: WHAT DOES THIS IMPLY?
Difficulty #1			
Difficulty #2			
Difficulty #3			

12. Source: *Methodical Bible Study* by Robert Traina, page 99+.

CHAPTER SEVEN
THE APPLICATION PROCESS

INTRODUCTION

Application is not the job of a pastor. Application is the response of the individual's heart to the spoken Word of God as the Holy Spirit communicates His truth. Of course, pastors and others may use illustrative applications in sermons or in times of sharing, but it is up to the individual (you and me!) to respond to the Word in obedience. We are each accountable to God. There is no good reason to study Scripture if it will not be applied.

James 1:22-25 gives us apt warning:

> Do not merely listen to the word, and so deceive yourselves. Do what it says. {23} Anyone who listens to the word but does not do what it says is like a man who looks at his face in a mirror {24} and, after looking at himself, goes away and immediately forgets what he looks like. {25} But the man who looks intently into the perfect law that gives freedom, and continues to do this, not forgetting what he has heard, but doing it--he will be blessed in what he does.

First Corinthians 2:9-10 says:

> However, as it is written: "No eye has seen, no ear has heard, no mind has conceived what God has prepared for those who love him" -- {10} but God

has revealed it to us by his Spirit. The Spirit searches all things, even the deep things of God."

Application follows interpretation. Interpretation asks the question, "What does this mean?" Application asks the question, "What does this mean to me/to us?" Application is the continuation of the process of study during which life and Word come together. Without this, all of the former parts are useless. Correct application must be based on accurate interpretation, and accurate interpretation must be based on correct observation! Observation and interpretation without application are merely intellectual exercises. Going to an extreme with only observation results in enlarged heads full of Bible facts and trivia. Facts without relationship to life have no meaning whatsoever. If one only does the application, how does one know that kind of thinking or behavior is biblical? If a person only makes interpretation, how can it be accurate if studying and observing the text are not part of the process? Application is the result of observation and interpretation.

PRINCIPLES OF APPLICATION

The following are some basic principles of application.

1. Never apply before you first observe and interpret.
2. Application is not a single event; it is a process.
3. Be in touch with your own strengths, weaknesses and needs.
4. Know the needs of the people around you when teaching so that appropriate application can be made.
5. If you are a teacher, reduce the passage to a principle or truth that is
   • relevant to students' needs.
   • consistent with the overall truth of God's Word.
   • general, yet specific enough to follow.
6. Evaluate the passage in light of your relationships: God, yourself, other believers, your work or school environment, your family, non-believers, government, etc.

What are the results of application? Listen to what Jeremiah said in 15:16:

When your words came, I ate them; they were my joy and my heart's delight, for I bear your name, O LORD God Almighty.

APPLICATION QUESTIONS

Various application questions can be used, but the primary question is, "What does it mean to me/to us?" Other questions would include:

1. What would Jesus have me to do in this situation?
2. So what? So what if God is all-knowing?
3. How does this truth affect my life today?
4. What can I do right now or tomorrow to apply the Word of God?
5. What is my most significant need in respect to the truth God has taught me?
6. What does this truth show me about God's character and about Himself?
7. What does this truth tell me about living?
8. What does this truth mean for me in my own life in the here and now?
9. What is it that God wants me to do?
10. What does this tell me about God and how am I to respond to Him?

What happens when there is no application? Many dangers lurk when this is not done. Some of the following could possibly happen.

1. The deception in thinking that knowing is enough.
2. Substitution of the emotional response ("I enjoyed that") for a volitional decision ("I will obey regardless of feelings").
3. Decline of spiritual growth.
4. Little or no retention because truth is not practiced.
5. An empty and superficial life without the substance of truth in the inner life that sustains and empowers.
6. A testimony that will be adversely affected.
7. Ineffective teaching results unless one has applied the truth to his/her life.

EXPLANATION OF APPLICATION WORKSHEETS

In order to facilitate application, the following chart summarizes the worksheets that encourage personal and group Bible study application.

NAME	FEATURES OF WORKSHEET	HOW TO USE
Appl. Wksht #1	This is the basic worksheet with directions on the worksheet.	Personal or group use, junior high and above.
Appl. Wksht #1	Same as above without directions.	(Same as above)
Appl. Wksht #1-B	More unstructured in design yet with the basic elements found in the previous two.	Adult groups may use, as this assumes more abstract thinking
Appl. Wksht #1-C	Using the basic ideas but with more focus on the action/response needed to be accomplished	Adult group use, groups that need encouragement to be specific in certain calls to action
Appl. Wksht #2	This worksheet uses thirteen application questions that are connected with the passage and then to life.	Upper elementary children to adults can use this. Some of the questions can be deleted if not supported by the passage. Select appropriate questions.
Appl. Wksht #3	This worksheet focuses on personal application with written responses using three questions.	Use with serious Bible study groups as it requires transparency and openness.
Appl. Wksht #4	This application is based on 2 Timothy 3:16-17 and asks five questions.	Best used with senior high and older groups when studying epistles and doctrine books.

EXERCISE

Look up the following verses and specify what each verse has to say about application.
- Ezra 7:10
- Ezekiel 33:30-32
- Luke 6:46-49
- 2 Timothy 3:15-17
- Hebrew 4:12-13
- Hebrew 5:14
- James 4:17

SURRENDER IS THE CORNERSTONE OF ALL APPLICATION.
Source: *Studying, Interpreting, and Applying the Bible*, pp. 268, 272

WORKSHEET

APPLICATION WORKSHEET #1 (WITH DIRECTIONS)
INSIGHT AND APPLICATION

Insight: "What has the Holy Spirit shown me?" This is a concise statement of the relationship between the observed facts and the Holy Spirit opening to you the meaning of His Word. An insight is NOT merely an opinion or a feeling ("I think" or "I feel"), but its source is the Scripture! God wants us to come to the place of I KNOW!

I see God ...

SOURCE: (References that God used in teaching you this insight. Quote what the verse said about that insight. This may be in one verse or in many verses. Many need to hear more than once the particular insight that God is saying!

SOURCES/REFERENCE	QUOTATION OF SCRIPTURE

Application: Application is the result of what God is revealing to us personally. Record what God is teaching you.

God is showing me ...

APPLICATION WORKSHEET #1
INSIGHT AND APPLICATION

Date:

Insight: I see God ...

SOURCES/REFERENCE	QUOTATION OF SCRIPTURE

Application: God is showing me ...

Date:

Insight: I see God ...

SOURCES/REFERENCE	QUOTATION OF SCRIPTURE

Application: God is showing me ...

APPLICATION WORKSHEET #1-B

INSIGHT "I see ..."	SCRIPTURE PASSAGES	APPLICATION "God is showing me that I ..."

WORKSHEET

APPLICATION WORKSHEET #1-C

INSIGHTS "I see God ..."	SCRIPTURE PASSAGES	APPLICATION "God is showing me ..."	ACTION ACCOMPLISHED	THOUGHT CHANGED

WORKSHEET

APPLICATION WORKSHEET #2

Date: **Scripture Passage:**

Is there a(n):

1. **Example** for me to follow?

2. **Victory** for me to gain?

3. **Command** for me to obey?

4. **Lesson** for me to learn?

5. **Sin** for me to confess and forsake?

6. **Promise** for me to claim?

7. **Blessing** for me to enjoy?

8. **New thought** about God, Jesus Christ, Holy Spirit?

9. **Attitude** to change?

10. **Prayer** to pray?

11. **Error** to avoid?

12. **Truth** to believe?

13. Something to **praise** God for?

APPLICATION WORKSHEET #3
PERSONAL APPLICATION WORKSHEET

The purpose of this worksheet is to make specific applications.

1. What impresses me the most?
   (Generally, as you study a book of the Bible, God, by His Holy Spirit, will lay some particular aspect or person on your heart. Pray that God will open your eyes to a specific response.)

2. Where do I fall short in this?
   (When God speaks to you about a particular aspect of His Word, record that weakness. Use the singular pronouns, i.e. I, me, etc.)

3. With God's help, what do I intend to do about this?
   (Write a plan of action that you will take to correct what is lacking. Build that quality into your life. This action may vary from writing a letter of apology to meditating on one of God's truths. Be specific. Once this is done, date it.)

WORKSHEET

APPLICATION WORKSHEET #4
APPLICATION BASED ON 2 TIMOTHY 3:16-17

[16]All Scripture is God-breathed and is useful for teaching, rebuking, correcting and training in righteousness, [17]so that the man of God may be thoroughly equipped for every good work.

Scripture studied:

What "doctrine" (teaching) does God want me to learn from this passage?

What conviction/reproof does this passage bring to my heart and life?

What needs to be corrected in my life?

What training needs to occur in my life for me to be adequately equipped?

As an end result, how does this finalize into "equipped for every good work"?

CHAPTER EIGHT

TANGENTS FROM THE BASICS

INTRODUCTION

This interactive Bible study method offers a solid foundation to "tangent off" in a variety of areas in order to dig deeper and increase understanding. This chapter continues to build on the foundation previously presented.

TOPICAL STUDIES

A topical study traces a particular subject or topic through portions of Scripture, portions of a book, or the entire Bible text. Topical studies and correlations are clearly related as topics emerge in further study of the Word. However, differences lie in the starting point. Correlations are inevitable as God teaches you related aspects from your studies of the Scriptures. Topical studies emerge through Scriptural studies. The theme chart (Chapter 3) introduces themes as topics that have surfaced repeatedly in that book of the Bible. Repetitions, from the second observation, aid the evolution of themes within your study. For example, one major theme of Philippians is joy. So, natural topics and themes come forth from God's Word without the pressure of forcing the Word to say something it does not say.

The topical study is similar to a word study but more comprehensive in that several words may give the total picture of what the Bible is saying about a particular concept. (See "Word Studies" for further information.) Both word and topical studies are complementary of each other. Remember, allow the Word to speak for itself. Be open to the Word and desire to know what it says about a topic without predetermined ideas.

Not only do we see "natural" topics emerge from Scripture, but the theme chart may reveal a topic that needs expansion into other books of the Bible. Herein arise "general " topics—topics that consist of a variety of generalities found in Scripture, such as, the work or character of God, the Christian walk, the nature of humankind, ministry, the Church, etc.

SOURCES FOR TOPICS

1. **Best source**: Theme chart and repetitions found from observation #2 give themselves to words, phrases and concepts that are innately within Scripture. Topical studies may begin by observing the themes and repetitions. Thus, the naturalness of the biblical passages reveals topics.

2. **Secondary Source**: General themes can be found within the Scripture by asking the general question, "What does this paragraph or chapter or book say about _____?" Ideas for general themes would include ministry, nature or attributes of God, names of God, sin, grace, love, blood, sacrifice, etc.

Caution: General topics may be too extensive or too general, and you may become lost in the process of what is important or the quantity of material. The first source is the BEST direction to go concerning topics.

REFERENCE TOOLS:

Good reference tools, such as the following, are very helpful when studying topics:

1. **Concordances.** All references are given in which the word is found; the Greek and Hebrew words can be investigated as to their meanings, alternate meanings, and root words.

2. **Topical Bible.** This has done much of the work already by assimilating all Scriptures and additional related references.

Caution: At some point in your study, write a definition of the topic, as you understand it. **Remember**, topics are to follow proper inductive study, never vice versa!

PROCEDURE FOR TOPICAL STUDIES:

1. Completion of the basic study of the passage that includes the observation exercises and the theme chart.
2. Review your work and identify a topical concept for further investigation beyond the passage studied.
3. Use reference tools that inform you where the topic or concept is located beyond the passage studied.
4. Organize your findings on the topic. The following are some organizing formats:
   - into sub-topics
   - into time periods
   - frequency
   - logically
   - comparatively
   - by contrast
5. Determine the truths to which God has opened your eyes.
6. Record your observations and insights.
7. Apply what you have learned.

On the following pages is an example of a concept first observed in Philippians, then sought elsewhere in the New Testament. A second page can be used for Bible study. Of course, you may adapt one to your own interests! Topical Worksheet #2 is an alteration of the first worksheet as it focuses on the significance, the "why" behind the text. This worksheet notes relationships, differences, and similarities within the topic as it is developed in the Scriptures. First, briefly state what the Scriptures say in the respective column. This may be an exact quote or a paraphrase. Then explain why this Scripture is important respective to this topic.

WORKSHEETS ONLINE
All of the worksheets in the book are available as full-sheet versions at the book web site. You can use these versions in the classroom or for your own study.

www.dennisfledderjohann.com

WORKSHEET

TOPICAL WORKSHEET #1: EXAMPLE
GENERAL TEXT CHART

Topic "following my example" — Found in Philippians 3:17 (study limited to NT)

REFERENCE	TOPIC	REFERENCE	TOPIC
Philip. 3:17	Paul: join with others in following my example (pressing on with Christ)	Titus 2:7	In everything set them an example by doing what is good.
John 13:15	Jesus: I have set you an example that you should do as I have done for you—foot washing.	Heb. 4:11	Make every effort to enter that rest, so that no one will fall by following their example of disobedience.
1 Cor. 10:6	These things occurred as examples	James 5:10	As an example of patience in the face of suffering, take the
1 Cor. 10:11	These things happened to them as examples—past history for us to learn from		prophets who spoke in the name of the Lord.
1 Thess. 1:7	Thessalonians became a model to all the believers in Macedonia and Achaia	1 Peter 2:21	Christ's suffering is a example to you (and us!)
		1 Peter 5:3	Elders, be examples to the flock
2 Thess. 3:7	You know how you ought to follow our example = Paul, Timothy and Silas	2 Peter 2:6	Sodom and Gomorrah is example of what is going to happen to the ungodly
2 Thess. 3:9	We did this ... in order to make ourselves a model for you to follow.	Jude 7	Sodom and Gomorrah serve as an example of those who suffer the punishment of eternal fire.
1 Tim. 1:16	Jesus might display unlimited patience as an example for those who would believe on Him.		
1 Tim. 4:12	Timothy—Don't let anyone look down on you because you are young, but set an example for the believers in speech, in life, in faith and in purity.		

Continued ...

TOPICAL WORKSHEET #1: EXAMPLE
GENERAL TEXT CHART

OBSERVATIONS

Topic can be divided into 3 categories:

1. "Follow by my example." Philip 3:17; John 13:15; 2 Thess. 3:7, 9. Direction in following someone is by looking at what that person does.
2. "Learn from past experiences." 1 Cor. 10:6, 11; Heb. 4:11; 2 Peter 2:6; Jude 7
3. "Be an example to others." 1 Thess. 1:7; 1 Tim. 1:16; 4:12; Titus 2:7; James 5:10; 1 Peter 2:21; 5:3. This is primarily a Pauline concept.

APPLICATION QUESTIONS:

- What kind of example am I to others?
- Is my example worthy to follow?
- What am I learning from the examples of others? What should I not be/do?

WORKSHEET

TOPICAL WORKSHEET #1
GENERAL TEXT CHART

Topic:

REFERENCE	TOPIC	REFERENCE	TOPIC

Observations:

Application:

WORKSHEET

TOPICAL WORKSHEET #2
TEXT AND SIGNIFICANCE CHART

Theme/Topic:

REFERENCE	WHAT THE TEXT SAYS	SIGNIFICANCE

Observations and Conclusions:

Application:

WORD STUDIES

Leroy's purchase of a new model sports car motivated him to take a country ramble. As this suburban driver was traveling the gravel roads in the hills of the Blue Ridge Mountains, he turned his car onto a narrow mountain road, going uphill. On one side was a twenty-foot drop to a sparkling mountain stream; the other side was the rocky, vine-covered wall. Slowly and cautiously he rounded a curve only to see a pig in the middle of the road! Brakes were applied, gravel scattered, the horn blasted, and the pig slowly ambled off to the side of the road. With renewed pressure on the accelerator, the car lurched forward, traveling up the narrow trail. Just around the next curve, he met a pick-up high-tailing it down the hill. He had just enough time to pull over to the abbreviated shoulder, and yell, "Pig!" The gray-haired farmer heard the exhortation as he flew by, turned his head and yelled back, "City-slicker!" Then, he rounded the curve and ... found what he had been looking for right in the middle of the road!

Words are important because they are the vehicles for conveying thoughts, feelings, and desires. How very interesting, then, should be the study of those "living words" in which the revelation of God Himself has been conveyed! Yet words, separated from their meanings and contexts, are just empty terms; instead of being vehicles of thought, they become substitutes for it. Words are not static. They change meanings with the passage of time. Many words used in the King James Authorized Version no longer possess the same English meaning that they did in 1611. For example, we no longer use "prevent" in the sense of "precede," or "carriage" in the sense of "baggage." Many of these meanings may be inferred from the context, but other changes might not be so readily noticed.

The need to know the meaning of Biblical words in their cultural context and their historical usage is the reason for specific word studies in Scripture. The study of a word found in a particular Scripture will lead to an awareness of the usage of that word in the same or differing ways in other Scriptures. Two elements must be kept in mind when doing a word study—the context and the intent of the author.

Where do you begin in choosing meaningful words to study? Words that are profitable for word studies are found in the second observation exercise. The question to ask is, "What words are frequently repeated?" Here is where to begin. As the basic foundational study is done, repetitions will grow naturally. Frequently used words are candidates for "word study." The word may be a familiar one, or it may initially appear unknown and insignificant. Another source for word studies is the occasional word stated only once or twice in a passage.

Remember the story above? The word must be understood in its context. A word may have various meanings, but the context determines its meaning. A single word is seldom an adequate guide to a biblical theme. A word study is only valuable as a means of enhancing and further understanding a given topic and passage. (Word studies and topical studies go hand-in-hand.)

GENERAL IDEAS FOR CONSIDERATION IN MAKING WORD STUDIES

1. Write your definition of the word.
2. Use a Bible dictionary to discover the definition of the term.
3. Use a Bible concordance to check its occurrences.
4. In what concentrated area is this word found? Is there a pattern? (A concordance will help.)
5. What is the root of the word? (Etymology—knowing how to use Greek or Hebrew is an asset!)
6. Are there variant English equivalent meanings?
7. What Greek/Hebrew words are used? Are all the same?
8. When studying a NT word, don't forget the OT word.
9. Identify the word according to its grammatical category: noun, pronoun, verb, adverb, adjective, preposition, conjunction, interjection, article. (Here again the Greek can be of benefit—case, gender, number, tense, person, mood, voice, etc.)
10. After studying the word, read the passages from two or three other translations to determine how they used the word. Compare the NASV with the NIV, the NKJV, etc.

BASIC QUESTIONS TO ASK WHEN DOING A WORD STUDY

1. How does the author use this word?
2. How do other authors use this word?
3. How do secular writings use this word?

REFERENCE TOOLS TO USE WHEN DOING A WORD STUDY

1. Concordance
2. An interlinear, Greek-English New Testament gives the Greek text accompanied by a literal translation of the text in English. The margin usually has a corresponding passage found in KJV, NIV, or RSV.
3. Word dictionaries, such as *An Expository Dictionary of New Testament Words* by W. E. Vine, give the meanings of words against a Greek background. Comments are

given on Biblical passages under arranged headings. By a helpful system of cross references, not only are Greek words given that are represented by one English word, but also which English words, if any, are used to translate each Greek word. For those who can utilize the Greek language, the *Theological Dictionary of the New Testament* by Kittel is very helpful.

4.   Bible encyclopedias (Further explanation and information of these and other references are included in Chapter 4 under "Contextual Background.")

SUMMARY OF PROCEDURE:

1.   An observational study of the book will reveal key words that can be studied. Focus on one of these words!

2.   Use one of the worksheets found on the following pages or make your own.

3.   Once the word study is completed, do not forget to make observations of your work by asking the following questions:
     *   How does the author use the word? How do other authors use the word?
     *   How do secular writers (e.g. Josephus, Philo, etc.) use the word?
     *   Now that this word has been compared with other contexts, what makes this usage unique?
     *   How does the etymology help in understanding the word?
     *   Is the word consistently used in the same way?

An example of a word study is found on the following page. This study originates from Philippians 2:8 with the word "humbled."

*   **Word:** "humbled" (found one time in Philippians)
*   **Word defined:** "To make low"
*   **Frequency:** 16 times in the NT
*   **Number:** Third person singular
*   **Verb Tense:** aorist indicative active
*   **English meanings:** "Lowly in spirit, lowly of mind, low state, to make low, to humble"

Conclusions:
*   Humility is a choice of obedience.
*   Relationship of humility to other themes, e.g. compassion and gentleness

WORD STUDY WORKSHEET #3: EXAMPLE
PHILIPPIANS 2:8

REF.	CONTEXT OF THE WORD WHAT THE TEXT SAYS	SIGNIFICANCE / OBSERVATIONS
Matt. 11:29	Take my yoke upon you and learn from me, for I am gentle and humble in heart, and you will find rest for your souls.	• different Greek word • "gentle" and "humble" connected • Jesus is speaking
Matt. 18:4	Therefore, whoever humbles himself like this child is the greatest in the kingdom of heaven.	• adults argue as to who is the greatest • seems to imply that children are generally humble while adults are not!
Matt. 23:12 Luke 14:11 Luke 18:14	For whoever exalts himself will be humbled, and whoever humbles himself will be exalted.	• adverse relationship between exalted and humbled • concept is found 3 times in Gospels
Luke 1:48, 52 (Mary's prayer)	"My soul glorifies the Lord . . . for he has been mindful of the humble state of his servant . . . He has brought down rulers from their thrones but has lifted up the humble."	• concept of exaltation and humility connected
2 Cor. 12:21	I am afraid that when I come again my God will humble me before you	• God humbles people
Eph. 4:2	Be completely humble and gentle; be patient, bearing with one another in love.	• related themes of gentle and humble • command to be humble
James 1:9	The brother in humble circumstances ought to take pride in his high position.	• appropriateness to humility
James 4:6, 10	But he gives us more grace . . . "God opposes the proud but gives grace to the humble." Humble yourselves before the Lord, and he will lift you up.	• contrasts here • command, imperative—no choice! • humility has an effect
1 Pet. 3:8	Finally, all of you, live in harmony with one another; be sympathetic, love as brothers, be compassionate and humble.	• compassion and humility connected • commands to do and to be
1 Pet. 5:5, 6	Young men . . . be submissive to those who are older . . .clothe yourselves with humility toward one another, because, "God opposes the proud but gives grace to the humble." Humble yourselves, therefore, under God's mighty hand, that he may lift you up in due time.	• 1 Pet. 5:5 is same as James 4:6. Verse 6 is similar to James 4:10

BIOGRAPHICAL STUDIES

As you read the Scripture, you will continually be in contact with people found in the narrative. In order to learn from their example, character qualities, life styles, and what they said and did must be investigated. Studying the life of a person, the relationship with or lack of relationship with God, obedience or lack of obedience to God, relationship to others, and the results of choices he/she made can have a powerful impact.

"Character" is a classical Greek term meaning "impress," a "distinctive mark." Thus, in a biographical study, look for the distinctive marks God has made on each life. The purpose of biographical studies is to see God's impression or lack of it upon each one!

When doing a biographical study, be aware that there may be more than one individual in Scripture with the same name, and that individuals may have more than one name. A Bible dictionary will help to eliminate possible confusion on characters with the same name! A complete study requires inductive study of all Scripture written by or to that character, as well as any record about him/her.

REFERENCE TOOLS FOR USE IN CHARACTER STUDIES
1. Bible dictionary
2. Concordance or topical Bible

PROCEDURE
There are several ways that biographical studies may be done. The following worksheets give alternatives in using different observation worksheets, and the following procedure is for general consideration.

1. Decide on a particular character you have observed in your inductive study.
2. Note the paragraphs in which he/she is located. This is simply done by referring to your first observation exercise worksheet, column 1, under "characters." A concordance or topical Bible will help to determine other places in which this character may be found.
3. Concepts to look for:
    *   Behavior, action—What did this person do? Can his/her behavior be categorized—evil or good, selfish or giving?
    *   Meaning of his/her name (A Bible dictionary may be helpful.)
    *   Repetition of truths or actions of this character.
    *   Early childhood, training, conversion, unique experiences, etc.

- Time period in which he/she lived.
- Failures, accomplishments in his/her life.
- Condition of spiritual life: prayer life, obedience, suffering, personal lessons learned from God, attitudes, responses, reactions, use of Scriptures, revelations, etc.

4. After you have first done your work, check external sources for additional information.
5. Organize your observations
   - Chronologically—birth to death
   - Major events in life
   - View of doctrines
6. Apply to personal life

The following page is an example of a biographical study on Timothy.

EXERCISE

Choose a Bible character you have studied; select one of the worksheets on the following pages and do a biographical study.

WORKSHEET

BIOGRAPHICAL WORKSHEET #1: EXAMPLE

Character's Name: Timothy   **Meaning:** "honoring God"

FACTS / ACTIONS WITH REFERENCES	CHARACTER QUALITIES IDENTIFIED	CONCLUSION POSITIVE / NEGATIVE / EFFECT
Acts 16:1+ Background, hometown, parents Acts 17:14-15 Timothy stayed at Berea, later left Acts 18:5; 19:22; 20:4 staying at places, traveling to places	"disciple" with good reputation Works with Paul in ministry Followed Paul's instructions	Mother-Jewish, Father-Gentile This was positive and negative. Paul circumcised Timothy—positive for Jewish ministry. Positive co-worker
1 Cor. 4:17 "Faithful in the Lord; he will remind you" 1 Cor. 16:10 "he is carrying on the work of the Lord"	Faithful Teaching gift Diligent and obedient to God	Positive—being fruitful to task
2 Cor. 1:1, 19 "Paul and Timothy, our brother, Jesus Christ preached by Timothy"	Teamwork/Cooperative Preaching ministry	Positive—not independent
Philip. 1:1"Paul and Timothy, servants of Jesus Christ" Philip. 2:19 send Timothy to you	Co-authors, team Desire to know, be informed	Positive—team player and co-worker
Col. 1:1 Timothy our brother	Co-authors, team	Positive
1 Thes. 1:1 Paul, Silas, Timothy 1 Thes. 3:2 "Timothy who is our brother and God's fellow-worker in spreading the gospel of Christ to strengthen and encourage you in the faith" 1 Thes. 3:6 Timothy reports back	Co-authors, team Ministry of encouraging	Positive—team player and co-worker
2 Thes. 1:1 "Paul, Silas, Timothy to church"	Co-authors	Positive—work with others
Rom. 16:21 "Timothy, fellow-worker"	Fellow-worker	Positive—not alone
Philemon 1 "Paul and Timothy, our brother"	Co-author	
Heb. 13:23 "our brother Timothy has been released"	possible suffering	Hardships in life
Observation/Conclusions	Dominant qualities: co-worker, not independent Faithful and diligent	Effect of dominant qualities: good worker, supporter, dependent on church body

(continued)

BIOGRAPHICAL WORKSHEET #1: EXAMPLE

Questions:

1. What professions are found in this person's life?
   Constant growth in co-ministry

2. How much material—entire book, several chapters, one chapter, one paragraph—
   is found on this character? What does this tell us?
   Two books written to him. Many references, parts of many chapters to/about him.
   Timothy, though not flamboyant, was certainly a strong pillar in the New Testa-
   ment church and its growth.

3. Is this person mentioned elsewhere? If so, where? (Use a concordance.)
   1 & 2 Timothy

4. Summarize observations. (Why did this person do what he/she did?)
   Positive person—Implication: a joy to work with; interdependent. A team player
   and close to Paul.

WORKSHEET

BIOGRAPHICAL WORKSHEET #1

Character's Name: **Meaning:**

FACTS / ACTIONS WITH REFERENCES	CHARACTER QUALITIES IDENTIFIED	CONCLUSION POSITIVE / NEGATIVE / EFFECT

Questions:

1. What professions are found in this person's life?

2. How much material—entire book, several chapters, one chapter, one paragraph— is found on this character? What does this tell us?

3. Is this person mentioned elsewhere? If so, where? (Use a concordance.)

4. Summarize observations. (Why did this person do what he/she did?)

BIOGRAPHICAL WORKSHEET #2

Not all parts of this outline will be relevant to every character.

Character's Name: **Meaning:**

1. **References**

2. **Family Background.** Parents, birthplace, geographical environment, dates of life.

3. **God's Call/Commission.** Events previous to, the event itself, qualifications for the call.

4. **Preparation.** Educational background, distinguishing characteristic of preparations.

5. **Reputation.** What authorities said, what godly people said, what wicked people said, what God said.

6. **Message and Life.** Summary statement of life and message, key verse that describes life, how did he/she die?

7. **Conclusion.** What factors shaped his/her life and thinking? What were positive qualities? What were negative qualities? What passions did he/she exhibit? What influence did he/she have on others?

8. **Application.** In what way is this character an example to me? What can I learn from his/her relationship with God?

BIOGRAPHICAL WORKSHEET #3
GENERAL QUESTION WORKSHEET

1. Who was this person and what information about him/her is available to us in the Bible? In other historical books and documents?

2. What crucial decisions were made by this person as an individual or by a group of which he/she was a member?

3. What were the causes with which this person was identified and tasks to which he/she devoted intelligence and energy?

4. What were the distinctive qualities of this person's character?

5. What part did this person play in the history of the people of God?

6. On the basis of what you have observed, what kind of personality profile would you give this character? Would you want him/her as a friend? Why?

WORKSHEET

BIOGRAPHICAL WORKSHEET #4
CHARACTER COMPARISON CHART[13]

QUESTION	CHARACTER #1:	CHARACTER #2:
1. How did he/she emerge as a character?		
2. Did he/she honor God or let Him down? What was the occasion?		
3. What were his/her aims and motives?		
4. How did this person treat people with whom he/she was in contact?		
5. How did he/she respond to treatment by others?		
6. What does this person teach us about the lessons he/she learned from God? About humankind?		
7. What can we see of the impressions of God's nature upon his/her personality?		
Conclusions and Applications		

13. Original source of idea is from *How to Study the Bible* by John B. Job, page 148.

BIOGRAPHICAL WORKSHEET #5

Character:

OBSERVATIONS OF CHARACTERISTICS	WHAT CAUSED THESE?	WHAT RESULTED FROM THESE?	SIGNIFICANCE

CHAPTER NINE

INTERACTIVE BIBLE ACTIVITIES TO USE FOR SMALL GROUP BIBLE STUDIES

OVERVIEW

The purpose of this chapter is to connect previously discussed worksheets used on the personal Bible-study level to small-group Bible study settings of two to twenty-five people. As groups become larger, dynamics change. (In large groups preaching tends to occur rather than teaching.) A group of twelve gives adequate opportunity for all to participate in a sixty-minute Bible study. Since chapter three, numerous worksheets and charts have been introduced that could be used for small-group Bible activities. For example, in the previous chapter a biographical worksheet could be used about Peter based on Acts 1-4. Or, an analysis of a paragraph could use the three-column approach with any text.

ADDITIONAL WORKSHEETS

Additional worksheets may be designed based on the direction and needs of the group, and the passage being studied. Examples are listed on the following page.

WORKSHEET	PAGE	DESCRIPTION	USE
OIA Worksheet	123	Combines the basics of interactive Bible Study into one chart	Use for small group investigation into a paragraph — encourage group discovery!
Observation Question Worksheet	124	Connects the main idea with the purpose of the passage with background knowledge and feelings. Opportunity given for additional input by the student.	Use with small groups to establish the emotional climate with purpose and background of the book—builds connections rather than seeing things in isolation.
Observation Chart for Stories (first one includes directions, second does not)	125–126	Outlines various elements that need investigation when studying stories.	Biblical genre that support this chart, such as Ruth, Jonah, specific stories with historical literature.
Observation on Emotions	127	Investigates the emotions—origins and effects—found in a passage.	Use when passage supports emotional aspects, such as found in Psalms.
Observations on Psychological Factors (First has directions, second one does not.)	128–129	Addresses various psychological factors present in situations, people, etc.	Use with selected passages that support this worksheet and with mature groups with trusting relationships.
Observations on Prayer (First one has directions, second one does not.)	130–131	Investigates prayers in Scriptures	Use with prayers, possibly some of the Psalms.

IDEAS FOR GROUP BIBLE STUDY ACTIVITIES

The following ideas can be used with small-group Bible studies for the purpose of having students participate in the observation process.

1. **Content Focus.** How many verses has the author used to describe a topic, idea, concept, event, situation, etc.? Often the quantity of material indicates the value of material. Ask, "What does this say? What does this imply?"

2. **Time Factor.** How much time has transpired in this verse? paragraph? chapter? book? What word or words give any indication of time ? If a time can be ascertained, what other important events were occurring at that time? What other important people were living at that time? How does this "time" help us with other parts of the book?

3. **Relationship Factor.** What are the relationships between verses, chapters, paragraphs, words, verb tenses, before and after events, etc.? How is the text arranged?

Look at the connectives (conjunctions), prepositions, clauses, pronouns, etc. Look for changes. Compare the beginning to the end of the book. How does the passage naturally divide?

4. **Omission Factor.** Why did the author select the material he did? Why was this included and not something else? If this had been omitted, would it imply a lack of importance? Why?

5. **People Factor.** What does the name mean? Has that name occurred before? If so, where? What do other Scriptures say about these people? What reputations do they have?

6. **Event or Historical Factor.** Has a similar event occurred at another time? What makes this event distinct from other events? What cause and effect does this event have in the flow of history?

7. **Geographical Factor.** What does the name of the place mean? How did it receive this meaning? What important events took place here? Where is it today? What is it like today? Has archeological study been done on this place? If so, what?

8. **Grammar Items.** Observe verbs, various parts of speech, moods, tense, etc. Compare grammar from one verse to another verse.

QUESTIONS FOR SMALL-GROUP BIBLE STUDIES

Questions to ask when you see:

1. Names of People
    *   What do their names mean?
    *   Have I seen them before? If so, where?
    *   What do other scripture tell me about these people?

2. Events or historical material
    *   Has a similar event occurred at another time?
    *   What makes this event distinct from other events?
    *   What cause and effect does this event have in the flow of history?

3. Places or Geographical material
   - What does this name mean?
   - How did it receive this meaning?
   - What important events took place here?
   - Where is it today? What is it like today?
   - Has archeological study been done on this place? If so, what?

4. Time or Chronological material
   - What month and year did this occur?
   - What other important events were occurring at this time?
   - What other important people were living at this time?
   - How does this "time" help us with other parts of this book?

CONNECTING LESSON OBJECTIVES WITH LESSON ACTIVITIES

The lists of verbs on the following pages connect lesson objectives with activities that can be done in small-group settings. It is divided into categories based on Bloom's taxonomy. Verbs in the list can be connected to activities.

CATEGORIES	VERBS IN LESSON OBJECTIVES		SUGGESTED ACTIVITIES	
Knowledge	Check Define Describe Drill Identify List Memorize Name Quote Read	Recognize Reproduce Review Show Spell State Tell Underline Write	Assignments Checklists Definitions Games Generalizations Guided practice Notes	Principles Puzzles Q & A Tests/Quizzes Vocabulary Worksheets
Comprehension	Abbreviate Arrange Ask Conclude Demonstrate Determine Discuss Draw Explain Extend Identify Interpret List Listen Locate Match	Observe Paraphrase Prioritize Prove Rearrange Relate Represent Research Retell Rewrite Search Show Substitute Summarize Symbolize Translate	Books Charts Debates Descriptions Dramatizations Drawings Events Films Interviews Magazines	Maps Models Newspapers Outlines Paintings Show & tell Stories Tapes Tests Word problems
Application	Chart Check out Classify Collect Combine Construct Decide Demonstrate Develop Discover Examine Experiment Explain Explore Facilitate Graph Hypothesize Illustrate	Implement Interview Manipulate Order Organize Paint Plan Practice Produce Prove Reconstruct Record Report Show Solve Specify Teach Use	Booklets Brochures Charts Collections Diaries Dioramas Discussions Graphs Illustrations Lessons Maps	Mobiles Models Note cards Photographs Puzzles Reports Samples Scrapbooks Sculptures Simulations Term papers

CATEGORIES	VERBS IN LESSON OBJECTIVES		SUGGESTED ACTIVITIES	
Analysis	Analyze Break down Categorize Classify Compare Contrast Debate Deduce Defend Differentiate	Discover Dissect Divide Group Investigate Order Prioritize Rank Rate Separate	Articles Criteria Debate Diagrams Essays Flow charts	Outlines Polls Questionnaires Reports Stories Surveys
Synthesis	Combine Conclude Construct Create Develop Devise Dramatize Forecast Formulate Hypothesize	Improvise Imagine Infer Invent Predict Question Redesign Rework Rewrite Synthesize	Advertisements Diagrams Formulas Inventions Models Machines Movies News articles Paintings Pantomimes Poems Products	Programs Radio dramas Recipes Scripts Simulations Slogans Songs Stories Structures Theories
Evaluation	Appraise Assess Choose Conclude Debate Decide Dispute Editorialize Evaluate Grade Judge	Justify Prove Rank Rate Reason Recommend Scale Select Speculate Suppose Verify	Articles Conclusions Editorials Evaluations Letters Opinions Panels Recommendations Reviews Surveys Values Verdicts	

WORKSHEET

OIA WORKSHEET

VERSES	OBSERVATION	INTERPRETATION	APPLICATION
One complete sentence or Single verse (be careful with just one verse) or paragraph or chapter	What does it say? Ask questions that a reporter would ask and allow the text to answer the questions. Who? (people, authors, background of authors, conceptual ideas) What? (actions, verbs, attitudes, events, etc.) Where? (places, direction, geographical information, etc.) Why? (reasons for actions, why did this happen, etc.) When? (time element—past, present, future, completed, continuous, etc.) How? (means, how something is done, said, etc.)	What does text mean? What did the author mean when he wrote this? What does the content—words, sentences, syntax, grammar, etc.—mean? What is the meaning of the context before and after? Which words dealing with culture could be researched? Which concepts need research in a Bible dictionary or encyclopedia? Which words need to be researched for meaning and understanding? Which external sources (commentaries) need to be consulted with which verses?	How does this work? How do I apply this to my life? What will I think/feel/do now that I understand this passage? I will . . . help, serve, learn, repent, start, stop, read, praise, thank, work, trust, share, forgive, give, go, run, walk, rest, apply, avoid, write, call, visit, etc.

WORKSHEET

OBSERVATIONS QUESTION WORKSHEET

MAIN IDEA	PURPOSE	BACKGROUND KNOWLEDGE	FEELINGS	MISC.
What is the main idea of this paragraph? State the main idea in one sentence using any repetitions that you see.	Determine the purpose of the passage by asking the question, "What is the purpose of this passage?" Passage could be a chapter or a paragraph.	What background knowledge is needed in order to understand this passage? If there is a person/place named, what is needed in order to know about that person or place? If there are new or important words, what do they mean?	What emotions and feelings are expressed? How did the character(s) feel?	Record other observations or questions here.

WORKSHEET

OBSERVATION CHART FOR STORIES[14]

GENERAL SETTING OF STORY	CHARACTERS IN STORY
• Make observations on place, environment, conditions, changes in the setting • What does the setting indicate/mean? • How does the setting contribute to action? • Are characters and setting the same for each scene? Explain.	• What do I know about the character from this story? • What does the action of this character tell me about this person? • Who is the protagonist (the main character around which the conflict of the story is built)? • Who is the antagonist (the forces who are against the protagonists)?
STORY ACTION: SUMMARY OF EVENTS	**PLOT CONFLICT**
• Summarize the beginning, the middle and the end events in one sentence. • What is the cause and effect relationship between the scenes? • Does action progress? • Does it repeat itself? (For example, the events of Jonah 1 would be the beginning, Jonah 2-3 the middle, and Jonah 4 the end.) • What is the story pattern? (Possible answers include the quest, a journey, death-rebirth, initiation, tragedy, a happy ending, crime and punishment, temptation, a rescue, etc.) • How does the pattern help us see the "Big Picture" of the book? • How much space is given to characters? Events?	• Identify the conflicts within the story. Are they physical? Are they between characters? Morals? Spiritual issues? Mental issues? Psychological issues? Environmental issues? Supernatural issues? • Is there more than one? • How is the conflict resolved?

INTERPRETATION
1. What does the story say about: (Note the positive (+) and negative (-) by using symbols.) • God • People • Life/Reality 2. How do the characters represent us? How should main characters' experiences be viewed? 3. What is the story an example of? 4. What perspectives are we to share with the writer?

APPLICATION
1. How have you "lived" the experiences of this story? When have you felt the same feelings as the characters did in this story? What was the final outcome? 2. If you had been the main character, what would you have done and why?

14. Ideas taken from *Effective Bible Teaching*, pp. 119-121, 207-221.

WORKSHEET

OBSERVATION CHART FOR STORIES

GENERAL SETTING OF STORY	CHARACTERS IN STORY

STORY ACTION: SUMMARY OF EVENTS	PLOT CONFLICT

INTERPRETATION

APPLICATION

WORKSHEET

OBSERVATIONS ON EMOTIONS WORKSHEET

SCRIPTURE	EMOTION IDENTIFIED	ORIGIN OF EMOTION	EFFECT OF EMOTION	COMMENTS, OBSERVATIONS, OR QUESTIONS
Record Scripture reference in this column	Identify the words that designate emotions/feelings in the passage. What is the emotion? Is it a general or specific emotion? Describe this emotion. Would this imply the presence of other emotions? If so, what might they be?	Do people belong to emotions? Connect the emotions with the appropriate person. What does this say about this person? What are the implications of the emotions in relationship to the person? What caused this emotion? What was God's role in this? Did some situation or circumstance produce this? Did the person produce it? Did the person have any control over this? If so, how much? Were there certain events that prompted this emotion?	Which of the emotions/feelings identified are positive? Negative? Are any emotions in the story condemned? If so, why do you think this is? If not, why not? What was the result? Was there any long-term effect? Any immediate effect? What effect did it have on the person? On others? On family? On strangers?	Do any of these emotions reflect God? In what way? Does God display His emotions? How does He display His emotions?

WORKSHEET

OBSERVATIONS ON PSYCHOLOGICAL FACTORS

The purpose of this worksheet is to record observations that deal with the psychological factors of situations, people, discourses, etc.

VERSES	PSYCHOLOGICAL FACTORS	IMPLICATIONS OF FACTORS	EFFECTS / RESULTS	CONCLUSIONS & COMMENTS
Record the passage that you are working on in this column.	Identify the words that designate psychological factors in the passage. How does this passage appeal to the mind/intellect? How does this passage appeal to the soul? How does this passage appeal to the imagination?	What motives are evident? What purposes or reasons are evident in this passage? What issues are addressing the inner needs of the soul? What does this say about this person? What are the implications of these factors in relationship to the person? What caused this? What was God's role in this? Did some situation or circumstance produce this? Did the person produce it? Did the person have any control over this? If so, how much?	What are the short-term effects of such factors? What are the long-term effects of such factors? Which of these factors are positive? Negative? What effect did it have on the person? On others? On family? On strangers?	What would possible psychological effects be to that specific person or to others? Do any of these emotions reflect God? In what way? Does God display His emotions? How does He display His emotions?

WORKSHEET

OBSERVATIONS ON PSYCHOLOGICAL FACTORS

The purpose of this worksheet is to record observations that deal with the psychological factors of situations, people, discourses, etc.

VERSES	PSYCHOLOGICAL FACTORS	IMPLICATIONS OF FACTORS	EFFECTS / RESULTS	CONCLUSIONS & COMMENTS

WORKSHEET

OBSERVATIONS ON PRAYERS

The purpose of this worksheet is to investigate the structure and elements of prayers as found in Scripture

SCRIP.	WHO IS PRAYING?	STRUCTURE OF THE PRAYER	REQUESTS MADE	GOD'S CHARACTER	PRAYER ANSWERED?
How many verses is this prayer? How long, in terms of minutes would this take to pray? What does the length indicate about the prayer?	Who is praying? What do you know about this person? What do you know about this person's prayer life? Does prayer characterize the person's life? What other prayers did he/she pray?	How does the prayer begin? How does it end? What is its flow— subject to subject, one item to another non-related item, etc.? Note the progression of subjects. Are any repeated? Is thanksgiving included? For what? For whom? Is worship or adoration included? Compare the ACTS model to this prayer. (Adoration, Confession, Thanksgiving, Supplication)	What specific requests are made? General requests? Is there prayer for a group of people? For an individual? How are they being prayed for? Compare the requests observed here with the requests you usually make.	How is God's character revealed in this prayer? What words/ phrases reveal His character? How many elements of God's character are included in this prayer? What does this say about God?	Was the prayer answered? If so, when? How can this prayer be used today?

WORKSHEET

OBSERVATIONS ON PRAYERS

The purpose of this worksheet is to investigate the structure and elements of prayers as found in Scripture

SCRIP.	WHO IS PRAYING?	STRUCTURE OF THE PRAYER	REQUESTS MADE	GOD'S CHARACTER	PRAYER ANSWERED?

30 PLUS METHODS TO USE
WHEN TEACHING THE BIBLE

METHOD	PURPOSE	DESCRIPTION
Assignment (Also called "seat-work," "written reports," or "home-work")	To gain information by studying before the lesson	Individual or group homework or class work
Biographical Reading	To gain information, insight and inspiration	Students read biographies of great Christian men and women and share their findings with the class
Book Report	To gain information and insight	Students read and summarize for the class the contents of a book or passage
Brainstorming	To collect many ideas or solutions without judgment of ideas	Class members suggest and list as many ideas as possible on a subject withholding evaluation until all ideas are presented
Buzz Group	To gain information, allow discussion and solve problems	Small groups (4-8), discuss a topic for a limited period of time often using guiding questions
Case Study	To analyze and solve problems in order to gain insight or apply truth	Description of real life problem situation is presented; the class then analyzes the problem and offers opinions and/or solutions to problem
Circle Response	To enable every person to express his/her opinion	The teacher asks an open question which asks for student opinion; each person in turn gives an answer
Creative Art	To express thoughts, feelings and beliefs	Class members draw their thoughts, beliefs or feelings about a subject; students share their drawings or class members try to interpret drawings; can also be done as a group
Demonstration (Also called "Experimentation" when the student is doing it)	To learn a particular task or skill	Students observe as teacher actively shows how to solve a problem, implement an activity, or demonstrate a skill. Then, students are given opportunity to practice what they have learned
Discussion	To engage student thinking or engender a response to an issue	Through the use of carefully formulated questions, the teacher leads a time of group interaction on a particular subject

METHOD	PURPOSE	DESCRIPTION
Drama	To gain information, allow for attitude change, inspire or discover potential applications through observation, participation and identification	A formal dramatic presentation of an event or situation; class members may participate or observe
Field trip	To gain first-hand experience or information	Students make a visit to a museum, church, home, or other appropriate locations
Groups: small, buzz	To gain information, allow discussion and solve problems	A large group divided into subgroups of 3 - 8 persons for a brief period of time to discuss a topic or a problem. Buzz groups are usually for the purpose of reporting back to the larger group. Small groups discuss a topic for a limited period of time often using guiding questions
Group Response Team	To gain information and clarify issues	All or several class representatives interrupt a speaker at times to request immediate clarification of issues
In-depth Bible Encounter	To examine one's life in relation to Scripture and apply Scripture to life	Each person writes a Bible verse or passage in his/her own words, shares what has been written and answers the question, "If I took this passage seriously, what would I have to do?"
Inductive Bible Study	To determine what a passage says, means and how it applies to life	A direct study of Scripture in which the person or group seeks to discover what the author is saying, why he said it, what it means and how to apply the central truth
Interview	To gain information from person and respond to that information	Opinions and facts given by person in response to questions and an open discussion follows
Lecture	To gain information, clarify ideas, challenge and motivate	A prepared verbal presentation by a qualified person most often using visual aids and advanced organizers
Lecture Forum	To gain information and clarify issues	A discussion that follows a lecture
Listening Teams	To gain information or insight through purposeful participation	A class is divided into several small group; each group listens to a speaker seeking answers to specific questions (different for each group); then all groups share answers to questions
Media Talk-back	To gain information and react to that information	Students view a film, then discuss it as a class

METHOD	PURPOSE	DESCRIPTION
Memorization or Recitation	To check learning or develop thinking skills	Class members memorize Scripture passages or other related material. A process of the teacher questioning the content, students responding, then teacher giving feedback
Neighbor Nudging	To engage every person in thinking and discussion	Class is divided into pairs who discuss a particular question for one or two minutes
Panel	To gain information and insights from resource persons	Several qualified people discuss a particular topic (see Expanding Panel Discussion above)
Practice Teaching	To gain skill and understanding	Students teach their own or another class
Projects	To develop research skills, writing skills and possibly relational skills when working with others	Study of a subject that may lead to an oral report
Provocative Questions	To arouse interest, motivate thinking, introduce or apply an idea	A few discussion-oriented, open-ended questions are used to engage student interest and participation
Questions and Answers	To clarify thinking and problems, gain information and find solutions	Teacher asks questions and students respond in short answers; an alternative approach is to have the class devise questions of greatest interest to them to ask the teacher or one another
Research and Report	To gain information through individual study and sharing with the group	A problem is presented to the class and research assignments are made; researchers share their findings at the end of the class or at the next class
Role-Playing	To solve problems, develop skills	A problem is acted out with individuals identifying as much as possible with the characters; a discussion of the situation follows
Role Reversal Role-Play	To enter into the feeling of another person	Similar to role-playing except the individuals switch roles and play the opposite part
Stories and Storytelling	To gain interest, clarify a truth, illustrate an idea or apply concepts	Teacher or a class member tells or reads a relevant, real-life or fictional story; students listen, respond, or even role-play.
Story—open-ended	To provoke interest and participation from students	Presents a problem for students to solve, e.g. What would you do?
Symposium	To gain information and new insights from a group of resource persons	A series of speeches are given by experts on selected aspects of a particular topic or issue
Testing, quizzes, etc.	To stimulate thinking and assess knowledge	Teacher requests written or oral responses to questions as a means of measuring learning

CHAPTER TEN

INTERACTIVE BIBLE STUDIES FOR CHILDREN

INTRODUCTION

"Sit still!" says Mrs. Jones, the Sunday School teacher for first graders.

"But I am tired of sitting still. Can't I do something?"

How often is this kind of conversation found when working with children? Their little bodies are saying, move, wiggle, and run yet the teacher wants them to be quiet and sit still. Are teachers in actuality fighting with God's design of children? There is something that can be done to channel their energy in a productive way.

The material which has already been given can easily be used for children ages 12 and above. Obviously, the parents would best know the appropriate age, as maturity and spiritual growth levels vary. But what about younger children? The purpose of this chapter is to offer numerous ideas on Bible studies for children, four years and older, readers and non-readers alike. Our attempt is to develop good observation skills within children, so they will see what is in Scripture and enjoy participating in the learning process of Bible study. Not all children will desire to do these things; our encouragement is to develop your own charts—fun, yet meaningful—and activities that your children will be enthusiastic about. Bible study is boring when you, as a parent, make it that way for your children. Use "opportune moments" in teaching your children God's truths and provide a structured opportunity for them to discover on their own the blessings and challenges of Bible study.

The following are various adaptations of charts for children to use. As you study God's Word and are an example to your children, God will give you ideas and insights for observation charts that you can make for your children.

USING PICTURES FOR OBSERVATIONS

Pictures can be used in various ways, and this activity for non-readers is adaptable. As the parent reads a chapter from the Bible, children illustrate what they hear. Once the chapter is read, have each child tell about his/her own picture. (A paraphrase or children's Bible is useful so they can understand the words.)

	DEFINITION	AGE LEVEL	NEEDS	DIRECTIONS
Chapter Picture	ONE picture for EACH chapter	2-3 and above	paper pencil or markers, children's Bible	Parent/teacher reads the chapter from children's Bible. As the chapter is read, the children draw what they hear. After the chapter is read, each child tells about the picture.
Picture Verse	ONE picture for ONE verse	4 and above	Paper pencil or markers, children's Bible	Write the verse on the top of the page, talk about the verse with the child, and then give the child time to illustrate the verse. Proverbs is an effective book to use for this.
Paragraph Pictures	ONE picture for ONE paragraph	5-6 and older	paper pencil or markers, children's Bible	Read a paragraph to your child, then have him/her draw a picture of that Scripture. Ask questions to determine what each one understood and learned. This is appropriate for books with flowing stories that the child can easily hear and understand, e.g. Jonah.

WORKSHEETS ONLINE

All of the worksheets in the book are available as full-sheet versions at the book web site. You can use these versions in the classroom or for your own study.

www.dennisfledderjohann.com

PICTURE VERSE

A gentle answer quiets anger but a harsh one stirs it up, Proverbs 15:1

Female   Age - 7½

WORKSHEET

PARAGRAPH PICTURES
ILLUSTRATION AND EXPLANATION

CHAPTER AND VERSES	CHAPTER AND VERSES
THIS IS DESIGNED FOR THE YOUNG READER! **Approximate ages: 7-9**	Purpose: To capture the essence of the paragraph in picture form, producing a continuous progression of the book in paragraph picture form.
CHAPTER AND VERSES	**CHAPTER AND VERSES**
Parents/Teachers: After the child has drawn the picture, have him/her share the "story" behind the picture.	Needed: • The child needs to be able to read his/her Bible, i.e. a children's Bible. In using his/her own Bible, the child realizes the worth and importance of the Word in his/her own life. • Colored markers or pencils work best for the child to draw colored pictures. • Instruct the child in the way paragraphs are designated in his Bible.
CHAPTER AND VERSES	**CHAPTER AND VERSES**
Bible books to use: (suggested list) • Gospels (Mark is a good one!) • Ruth • Esther • Any other book you believe would work well, but make sure the book uses concrete terms so that pictures can be drawn. Here is an example of a paragraph drawn by an eight-year-old child. The reference gives the book, chapter and verses. Has the essence of the paragraph been captured?	 MARK 4:35-41

- Place each completed sheet in a notebook, developing your child's own Bible study notebook that can later be used for reference and study.
- Please photocopy the chart on the next page for your child's use!

WORKSHEET

CHILDREN'S OBSERVATION CHART
FOR CHARACTERS AND TITLES

Book:

CHAPTER	MAIN CHARACTERS	CHAPTER TITLE

Approximate ages: 9 and up

- **Books of the Bible:** Any book which has characters would be appropriate, e.g. Jonah, Ruth, a gospel, Joshua, Acts, Genesis, historical books in the Old Testament, etc.
- **Purpose:** To identify the main characters in the chapter and to summarize the general idea of the chapter using a title.
- **Parents:** Once your child has completed the chart by chapter or book (whichever you decide), have him/her share with you discoveries and observations. Ask questions about why he/she recorded specific things!

WORKSHEET

CHILDREN'S OBSERVATION CHART FOR IDENTIFYING CHARACTER QUALITIES

Book:

CHAPTER NUMBER	PLACE: WHERE DID THE EVENTS TAKE PLACE?	CHARACTER QUALITIES: WHAT CHARACTER QUALITIES DO YOU SEE?	MOST DESIRABLE QUALITIES: WHICH DO YOU DE-SIRE AND WHY?

Approximate ages: 8-10

- **Purpose:** To focus on the characters in the Bible and the KIND of people they were, answering questions such as the following:
  1. What kind of people were they?
  2. What do I like about them?
  3. What do I not like about them?
  4. What character qualities are evident in their lives?
  5. Where do I see this?
- **Parents/Teachers:** After your child has completed the chart or has done a chapter, give time for sharing discoveries and observations. Ask specific questions. e.g. What effect does the place/situation/environment have on the character and the kind of person he/she was?
- **Bible:** Books of the Bible to use: Gospels, Ruth, Esther, Judges, 1 and 2 Samuel, or any book of the Bible with leading characters, whether one or many.

WORKSHEET

CHILDREN'S OBSERVATION
WHO/WHAT CUE

Book:

CHAPTER / PARAGRAPH	WHO? PEOPLE	WHAT? ACTION	SUMMARY STATEMENT
Record the chapter or portion of Scriputre by paragraphs	Who are the characters you find in this chapter or paragraph?	What is happening? What are the characters doing or saying?	In one sentence summarize the paragraph/chapter.

Approximate ages: 10-12. This is an adaptation of the original observation chart.

- **Purpose:** To develop insight into more Scripture details while also seeing the larger picture of the book.
- **Parents/Teachers:** Continue to talk about what your child is seeing, to ask questions, and to encourage.
- **Bible:** One of the gospels, or another book that has action and moves along, would work here, i.e. Genesis.

CHILDREN'S TOPICAL OBSERVATION CHART

Book:

CHAP./PARAGRAPH	TOPIC	INFORMATION	IMPORTANCE
Explanation: Chapter/Paragraph: Identify the chapter or the paragraph, depending on what you are working on.	Note the major subjects found in the book.	The question being answered is, "What is being said about the topic/subject of _____? Write your answer in this space.	Significance: The question being answered is, "Why is this important?" or "What meaning does this have?"

Approximate ages: 10-12.

- **Purpose:** To introduce themes found in the Bible and in specific books of the Bible.
- **Parents and or Teachers:** This may be difficult for your child. If you see that he/she is having trouble with these questions, use the "Who/What Cue."
- **Books of the Bible:** Letters of New Testament, for example, Philippians, Philemon, or 1 John.

SUMMARY OF CHAPTER

WHAT CAN A CHILD DO FOR BIBLE STUDY?

WHAT TO LOOK FOR	WHAT TO LISTEN FOR
Repeated words and phrases	Repeated words and phrases
People and proper names of people	Unusual or interesting sounding words
Places on a map	People and proper names of people
Questions asked	Geographical names
Questions not answered	Questions asked
	Questions not answered
	Potential sounds that could be found in text

OVERVIEW OF STUDY AIDS FOR CHILDREN

CHAPTER/IDEA/TITLE	SUGGESTED AGE LEVELS
Chapter Pictures	2-3
Picture Verses	4 and above
Paragraph Pictures for the non-reader	5-6 and older
Paragraph Pictures for the reader	7-9
Children's Observation Charts Characters and Title	9 and older
Character Qualities—Chart for Identifying Character Qualities	8-10
Who/What Cue—Children's Cue 1 Chart	10-12
Topics—Children's Topical Observation Chart	10-12

ANNOTATED BIBLIOGRAPHY

Ecclesiastes says, "Of making of many books there is no end" (12:12b KJV), and that is certainly true with books on the discipline of Bible study. I have found the following resources to be helpful in my Bible study journey. The annotated list cites books that have been most helpful to me over the years. These books have also offered help to many people who have found Bible study to be beneficial in their lives.

- Arnold, Jeffrey. *Discovering the Bible for Yourself.* Downers Grove, IL: InterVarsity Press, 1993. Out of print.

    Arnold's 151-page book on inductive Bible study uses Philemon as an example. His step-by-step approach to Bible study is applied to small group Bible studies with many practical dig-in-the-Word group exercises. His explanation of the inductive Bible study method is worthy of reading.

- Arthur, Kay. *How to Study Your Bible: The Lasting Rewards of the Inductive Approach.* 1994. Eugene, OR: Harvest House Publishers, 2010. Print.

    Kay Arthur, a popular writer in the area of inductive Bible studies, wrote this instruction manual as part of Precept Ministries. The book articulates many aspects of inductive Bible study, including observations using word studies, tense, voice and mood of verbs, and Bible study tools.

- Balchin, John F., David H. Field, and Tremper Longman III. *The Complete Bible Study Tool Kit.* Downers Grove, IL: InterVarsity Press, 1991. Out of print.

  This 400-page book attempts to bring together many dynamics of Bible study. It gives overviews, summaries, and explanations on customs and manners, plus hints on Bible reading, study, and interpretation. It is a combination handbook and customs/manners study tool.

- Barber, Cyril J. *Unlocking the Scriptures: The Key to Inductive Bible Study.* 2001. Eugene, OR: Wipf and Stock, 2004. Print.

  Barber uses the lives of Abraham and Sarah to demonstrate various Bible study techniques, which include the synoptic (overview), analytical, geographical, historical, cultural, doctrinal, biographical, ethical, devotional, and topical methods. Over two hundred pages give detailed descriptions for students desiring to understand the Bible.

- Bauer, David R. and Robert A. Traina. *Inductive Bible Study: A Comprehensive Guide to the Practice of Hermeneutics.* Grand Rapids: Baker Publishing House, 2011. Print.

  This masterful and comprehensive volume on inductive Bible study leaves few unanswered questions in the discipline of Bible study. It expands Traina's original work, though the basic framework is still evident. This volume is for serious Bible study students.

- Baughman, Ray E. *Creative Bible Study Methods: Visualized for Personal and Group Study.* Chicago: Moody Press, 1976. Out of print.

  Baughman uses the basic inductive design of observation, interpretation, and application but with different terms—say, mean, and apply. His attempt to visualize study tools is helpful. He shares ideas for group Bible study in visual formats.

- Berkhof, Louis. *Principles of Biblical Interpretation.* Grand Rapids: Baker Book House, 1950. Print.

  This is a classic book on understanding the Bible. Though the writing style is somewhat out-of-date, the content is still relevant.

- *Bible Studies Handbook.* 1980. Colorado Springs: Navpress, 1994. Print.
  This handbook is an overview of popular Bible studies used in Navigator resources. It touches on the inductive method in various forms. Examples and
  charts help clarify types of Bible studies. The appendix suggests a long-range
  Bible study program.

- Braga, James. *How to Study the Bible.* Portland, OR: Multnomah, 1982. Out of
  print.
  This detailed how-to book deals with multiple approaches to Bible study,
  particularly cultural, doctrinal, and typological methods. The author explains
  each step using appropriate charts, and concludes with an assignment whose
  answers can be checked in the back of the book.

- Briscoe, D. Stuart. *Getting in God.* Grand Rapids: Zondervan, 1975. Out of print.

- Brown, Michael Joseph. *What They Don't Tell You: A Survivor's Guide to Biblical
  Studies.* Louisville: Westminster John Knox Press, 2000. Print.
  Brown desires to assist students in understanding the discipline of biblical
  studies by giving twenty-eight common practices for biblical interpretation.
  These range from "Get a map" to "Don't argue what you can't prove." His
  academic approach includes few references to the Holy Spirit's ministry in the
  interpretation process. It lacks practicalities of observation.

- Duvall, J. Scott and J. Daniel Hays. *Grasping God's Word.* 2001. Grand Rapids:
  Zondervan, 2005. Print.
  According to the sub-title, this comprehensive book is a hands-on approach
  to "reading, interpreting, and applying the Bible." Duvall and Hays' 462-page
  volume has three appendices as well as an application exercise at the end of each
  chapter. This is not a book for beginning Bible students, as details and terminol-
  ogy would probably discourage comprehension.

- Fee, Gordon D. and Douglas Stuart. *How to Read the Bible for All Its Worth.* 3rd ed.
  Grand Rapids: Zondervan, 2003. Print.
  This popular book has been recently revised. It addresses various Bible
  genre—epistles, Old Testament narratives, historical passages, parables, wis-

dom literature, prophets, and revelation. Examples, illustrations and application questions are included. This is a comprehensive study in 287 pages.

- Finzel, Hans. *Unlocking the Scriptures: A Fresh, New Look at Inductive Bible Study.* 1986. Colorado Springs: D. C. Cook, 2003. Print.
  This is a well-written book with personal exercises for student interactions.

- Gettys, Joseph M. *How to Enjoy Studying the Bible.* Richmond, VA: John Knox Press, 1967. Out of print.
  One of the first books about Bible study methods, this classic is still one of the best as an introduction to various methods.

- Griffith-Thomas, W. D. *Methods of Bible Study.* 1975. Charleston, SC: Nabu Press, 2011. Print.
  Though the title indicates "methods" of Bible study, this classic is really an introduction to the Bible, giving a survey of the Bible itself, Old Testament books and outlines, and New Testament books and outlines as it attempts to address the value and importance of Bible study. According to the Baptist Bible Believer's website, this book was first published in 1903.

- Hall, Terry. *Getting More from Your Bible.* Wheaton, IL: Victor Books, 1984. Out of print.
  This easy-reading book covers various aspects of Bible study. It contains excellent ideas for making Bible study engaging, and practical ideas for appropriating God's truth into one's study life and into everyday life! (The 1982 title of this book was *Off the Shelf and Into Yourself.*)

- Hendricks, Howard G. and William D. Hendricks. *Living by the Book.* 1996. Chicago: Moody Press, 2007. Print.
  Written by a well-known Christian educator and his son, this book explains in detail all aspects of the inductive tool (392 pages) mixed with life stories that make reading enjoyable. Short chapters make the book an easy read.

- Henrichsen, Walter, and Gayle Jackson. *Studying, Interpreting, and Applying the Bible.* Grand Rapids: Zondervan, 1990. Print.

- Houghton, Frank; et. al. *Quiet Time: An InterVarsity Guidebook for Daily Devotions.* 1945. Downers Grove, IL: InterVarsity Press, 1980. Out of print.

  The book gives practical suggestions for practicing quiet time. Some are applicable for Bible study.

- Jensen, Irving L. *Enjoy Your Bible.* 1969. Wheaton, IL: Harold Shaw Publishers, 1992. Out of print.

  This is a short, concise, easy-to-read book on ideas for the basics of Bible studies.

- ———. *Independent Bible Study.* Chicago: Moody Press, 1974. Out of print.

  In this introductory text, Jensen gives the means to do-it-yourself Bible study. His strengths are in helping students analyze portions of Scripture by asking questions that unlock the texts' meaning, and in helping them visualize truths with outlines, charts, maps, and diagrams. Jensen's earlier book—*Inductive Bible Study: A Guide to Personal Study of the Scripture* (1963)—contains similar content.

- Job, John B., ed. *How to Study the Bible.* Downers Grove, IL: InterVarsity Press, 1973. Out of print.

  This is an introduction to methods of Bible study. Job's list does not include the inductive method, but various authors have discussed other methods— "Analyzing a Book," "Root Study," "The Bible and Contemporary Issues," etc.

- LaHaye, Tim. *How to Study the Bible for Yourself.* 1976. Eugene, OR: Harvest House, 2006. Print.

  This popular book deals with ideas for Bible study, from how to read to ways of studying the Bible by chapters.

- Leigh, Ronald W. *Direct Bible Discovery.* Nashville: Broadman Press, 1982. Out of print.

  Leigh believes that many Christians read books about the Bible but never get into the Bible itself. Therefore, he has written this inductive guidebook, which explains the principles and step-by-step procedures to help students discover correct interpretations of the Bible on their own. The author's website offers his book and additional information (www.ronleigh.com).

- Lincoln, William C. *Personal Bible Study*. Minneapolis: Bethany Fellowship, 1975. Out of print

  This is an excellent and thorough explanation of the inductive process. As a student of Robert Traina, the author blends much of the content with Traina's book; yet he includes further insight and simpler descriptions and explanations than does Traina.

- McQuilkin, J. Robertson. *Understanding and Applying the Bible*. Chicago: Moody Press, 1983. Print.

- Mikelson, A. Berkley. *Interpreting the Bible*. Grand Rapids: Eerdmans, 1963. Print.

- Moody, D. L. *Pleasure and Profit in Bible Study*. Chicago: The Bible Institute Colportage Association, n.d. Out of print.

  Pre-dating Moody Press, this book was published by D. L. Moody. Though over 100 years old, it still contains relevant ideas. He makes the point that "word and work make healthy Christians." Both are needed; the Word alone results in spiritual FAT, but Work alone results in burnout, or falling into sin.

- Perry, Lloyd and R. Culver. *How to Search the Scriptures*. Grand Rapids: Baker Book House, 1967. Out of print.

- Ramm, Bernard. *Protestant Bible Interpretation*. 3rd ed. Grand Rapids: Baker Book House, 1970. Out of print.

- Ramsey, George H. *Tools for Bible Study*. Anderson, IN: Warner Press, 1971. Print.

- Richards, Lawrence O. *Creative Bible Study*. Grand Rapids: Zondervan, 1974. Out of print.

  Unlike other Bible study books, Richards' emphasis is not so much on methods or principles of objective interpretation, as upon the subjective aspects of previous perspectives and assumptions. He attempts to involve the readers with other people in the context of a small group to rediscover God's Word for themselves. Excellent illustrations and examples are included.

- *Search the Scriptures: An Approach to Chapter Analysis Bible Study.* Colorado Springs: Navpress, 1974. Print.

- Smith, Wilbur M. *Profitable Bible Study.* 2nd ed. Boston: W.A. Wilde Company, 1953. Out of print.

    This revised edition gives general information about Bible study, ranging from "Seven Great Things the Study of the Bible Will Do for Us" to "Books for the Bible Student's Library."

- Souter, John C. *Personal Bible Study Notebook.* (2 vol.) Wheaton, IL: Tyndale House, 1973 and 1976. Print.

- Sproul, R.C. *Knowing Scripture.* 1978. Downers Grove, IL: InterVarsity Press, 2009. Print.

    The uniqueness of this book is its emphasis on interpretation. Groundwork is laid as to why we need to study the Bible. In simple terms, Sproul presents the science of interpretation, giving practical guidelines for applying this science.

- Sterrett, T. Norton. *How to Understand Your Bible.* Downers Grove, IL: InterVarsity Press, 1974. Print.

    This excellent book builds and develops the area of understanding or interpretation in Bible study. The author presents general rules for reading the Bible and special principles for understanding different types of language, such as parables and allegories.

- Sun, Ruth. *Personal Bible Study: A How-to.* Chicago: Moody Press, 1982. Out of print.

    This is a short book dealing with Bible study as a head and heart function. Especially helpful are the categories of interpretive questions.

- Terry, Milton S. *Biblical Hermeneutics.* 2nd ed. Grand Rapids: Zondervan, n.d. Out of print.

    This classic was first published in 1898 and is now available on-line.

- Thompson, David L. *Bible Study that Works*. 1982. Anderson, IN: Warner Press, 2011. Print.

  This short, concise book is a simplification and combination of basic Bible study techniques as found and expanded in works by Traina, Lincoln, and Jensen.

- Torrey, R. A. *The Importance and Value of Proper Bible Study*. 1921. Charleston, SC: Nabu Press, 2009. Print.

  This book is composed of four sermons that Torrey gave at his Los Angeles church on Bible study topics—its importance and value, mode of interpretation, and promises that God has given.

- Traina, Robert A. *Methodical Bible Study*. Wilmore, KY: Asbury Theological Seminary, 1952. Out of print.

  This is the standard, in-depth, scholarly introduction to inductive Bible study. It is not for beginning Bible students; however, for serious students of the English Bible, this book is a must.

- Vos, Howard F. *Effective Bible Study*. Grand Rapids: Zondervan, 1972. Out of print.

  This is a guide to sixteen study methods. Academic in style, it was designed with college students in mind. The inductive method is the first of sixteen techniques mentioned. Others include the Rhetorical Method, the Cultural Method, the Political Method, etc.

- Wald, Oletta. *The New Joy of Discovery*. 1956. Minneapolis: Augsburg-Fortress Press, 2002. Print.

  Whereas Traina's book is the standard textbook, Wald's text is a workbook—teaching students to apply basic principles of inductive Bible study.

- Warren, Richard. *12 Dynamic Bible Study Methods*. Wheaton, IL: Victor Books, 1983. Out of print.

  As the title indicates, this book explains different ways to study the Bible—devotional, character quality, book background, etc. Many helps, ideas, and illustrations are given, including appendices.

- Wilhoit, Jim, and Leland Ryken. *Effective Bible Teaching*. Grand Rapids: Baker
  Book House, 1988. Print.

     This excellent book communicates the use of inductive Bible study in becoming
     an effective teacher of the Word. It focuses on study and teaching, whereas this
     Handbook primarily addresses how to study.

- Yohn, Rick. *First Hand Joy*. Colorado Springs: Navpress, 1982. Print.

DENNIS FLEDDERJOHANN, Ph.D., is chair of the Department of Educational Ministries at Moody Bible Institute in Chicago, Illinois. He taught at several colleges and served as pastor in churches in Georgia, Indiana, Illinois and North Dakota. Besides His Word, God has used Dennis' wife, Elizabeth, and their four adult children to teach him about Himself. Dennis earned a Ph.D. in Curriculum and Instruction from Loyola University of Chicago, master's degrees from Trinity Evangelical Divinity School and McCormick Theological Seminary, and a bachelor's degree from Toccoa Falls College.

WORKSHEETS ONLINE

All of the worksheets in the book are available as full-sheet versions at the book web site. You can use these versions in the classroom or for your own study.

www.dennisfledderjohann.com

CPSIA information can be obtained at www.ICGtesting.com
Printed in the USA
LVOW07s0409211213

366289LV00001B/125/P